# ZONDERVAN
# BIBLE
# STORYBOOK

God's relationship with man, as told in the Bible, is probably the most widely known story in the world. In the standard versions, it is not an easy story for children to read or understand. Here, with a sensitivity and regard for the original, the stories are retold in simple language enriched by evocative illustrations, which will make it available and meaningful to many thousands of children worldwide.

Jenny Robertson, *the author of* Zondervan Bible Storybook, *is married with two children. Jenny spent her childhood in the East End of Glasgow. She graduated from Glasgow University and spent a year in Poland studying at the University of Warsaw. Jenny's interest in Jewish and Old Testament customs dates from this time. Back in Scotland, she became a school social worker and this experience has given her a particular understanding of her child readership. Jenny has had three children's novels published and also wrote the text for Scripture Union's* Encyclopedia of Bible Stories *and the Ladybird* Bible books.

Alan Parry, *who illustrated* Zondervan Bible Storybook, *is married with three children. He gained his National Diploma in Design at the Hornsey College of Art in North London, and became a freelance illustrator thirteen years ago after a spell in advertising. He has specialized in figure illustration and particularly enjoys researching and drawing historically accurate costumed figures.*

Robertson, Jenny.
   [Ladybird Bible storybook]
   Zondervan Bible storybook / text by Jenny Robertson, incorporating the "God's story" script by Oliver Hunkin, in association with Yorkshire Television ; illustrated by Alan Parry.
   p.   cm.
   Previously published as: Ladybird Bible storybook. 1983.
   Summary: Presents stories from the Bible retold in simple language.
   ISBN 0-310-44430-6
   1. Bible stories, English.   [1. Bible stories.]   I. Parry, Alan, ill. II. Title.
BS551.2.R53 1988
220.9'505—dc19
          88-20442
          CIP
          AC

Script copyright 'God's Story' © Yorkshire Television MCMLXXX
Text © Scripture Union MCMLXXXIII
Illustrations © Scripture Union MCMLXXXIII

First published 1983
by Scripture Union, 130 City Road, London, EC1V 2NJ
ISBN 0-7214-7525-6
Formerly published by Zondervan as The Ladybird Bible Storybook
Zondervan Publishing House,
1415 Lake Drive, S.E.,
Grand Rapids, Michigan 49506

*Printed in the United States of America*

88  89  90  91  92  93 / DH / 12  11  10  9  8  7  6  5  4  3

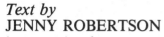
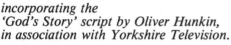

# ZONDERVAN BIBLE STORYBOOK

*Text by*
**JENNY ROBERTSON**
*incorporating the*
*'God's Story' script by Oliver Hunkin,*
*in association with Yorkshire Television.*

*Illustrated by*
**ALAN PARRY**

Zondervan Books
Zondervan Publishing House
Grand Rapids, Michigan

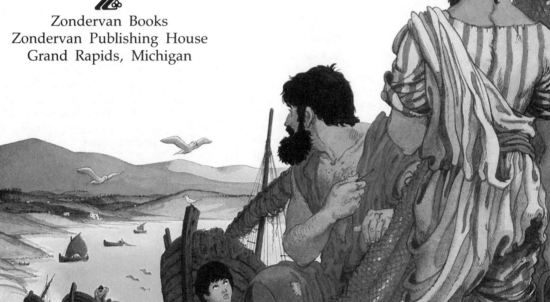

# Old Testament Contents

**In the Beginning**

| | |
|---|---|
| The Creation | 4 |
| The Garden of Eden | 9 |
| The cunning snake | 10 |
| A friendship spoilt | 12 |

**Safe in the Ark**

| | |
|---|---|
| Cain and Abel | 14 |
| Noah builds a boat | 16 |
| The flood | 19 |

**Abraham's Family**

| | |
|---|---|
| Abraham goes on a long journey | 24 |
| The Promised Land | 26 |
| God's promise comes true | 29 |
| Rebekah and Isaac | 33 |
| Jacob and Esau | 36 |
| Jacob steals the blessing | 37 |
| Jacob's dream | 39 |
| Laban cheats Jacob | 41 |
| The brothers make friends again | 43 |

**Joseph**

| | |
|---|---|
| The favourite son | 44 |
| Joseph the slave | 48 |
| Joseph in prison | 50 |
| Pharaoh's strange dreams | 51 |
| Joseph and his brothers | 54 |
| A test of loyalty | 58 |

**Moses the Prince**

| | |
|---|---|
| The baby in the basket | 60 |
| Moses runs away | 62 |
| Moses and the burning bush | 63 |
| Moses and Aaron go to see the king | 65 |
| Disaster in Egypt | 69 |
| Escape from Egypt | 71 |

**Moses and Joshua**

| | |
|---|---|
| Food in the desert | 75 |
| Laws at Mount Sinai | 76 |
| Aaron makes a gold bull | 78 |
| The Tent of God's Presence | 79 |
| The spies' story | 81 |
| Forty years in the desert | 82 |
| Joshua, the new leader | 85 |
| Crossing the Jordan | 86 |
| Victory in Jericho | 88 |

**Gideon**

| | |
|---|---|
| A mighty hero | 90 |
| Gideon and the sheepskin | 93 |
| Gideon's small army | 94 |

**Samson**

| | |
|---|---|
| Invaders from the sea | 98 |
| Samson's riddle | 99 |
| Samson is betrayed | 102 |

**Ruth**

| | |
|---|---|
| Famine in Israel | 106 |
| Ruth and Boaz | 108 |

**Samuel**

| | |
|---|---|
| Hannah's promise | 111 |
| A voice in the night | 113 |
| Capture of the covenant box | 114 |

**Saul**

| | |
|---|---|
| The people ask for a king | 116 |
| Saul becomes king | 118 |
| Saul disobeys God | 121 |

**David the Shepherd King**

| | |
|---|---|
| God chooses a new king | 123 |
| David at the palace | 124 |
| David kills Goliath | 127 |
| Saul the jealous king | 132 |
| Jonathan warns his friend | 134 |
| David spares Saul's life | 135 |
| Saul's last battle | 136 |
| King David captures Jerusalem | 138 |
| Feasts and dancing in the streets | 140 |
| David and Bathsheba | 142 |

**King Solomon**

| | |
|---|---|
| Solomon's coronation | 144 |
| Solomon's dream | 145 |
| A problem for Solomon | 147 |
| Building God's Temple | 148 |
| The visit of the Queen of Sheba | 152 |
| Solomon's power and wealth | 154 |
| The kingdom is divided | 157 |

**Elijah and Elisha**

| | |
|---|---|
| Elijah warns King Ahab | 160 |
| Elijah meets a poor woman | 162 |
| Contest on Mount Carmel | 164 |
| God speaks to Elijah | 167 |
| A new helper for Elijah | 169 |
| The rich woman's son comes back to life | 172 |
| Elisha and the poisoned stew | 173 |
| Naaman is healed of leprosy | 174 |

**Jeremiah**

| | |
|---|---|
| God's special messenger | 176 |
| Jeremiah is laughed at | 177 |
| Jeremiah is arrested | 180 |
| Jeremiah won't give up | 180 |
| The siege of Jerusalem | 183 |
| Jeremiah in the dungeon | 185 |
| Jeremiah buys a field | 188 |
| Jeremiah's last journey | 190 |

**Daniel and Esther**

| | |
|---|---|
| A special diet | 191 |
| Nebuchadnezzar's dream | 192 |
| Into the furnace | 193 |
| Daniel and the lions | 195 |
| Esther is made queen | 198 |
| Plots in the palace | 200 |
| Esther risks her life | 202 |
| Mordecai is rewarded | 202 |
| The enemy is discovered | 204 |

**God's Builders**

| | |
|---|---|
| Back to Jerusalem | 206 |
| Rebuilding the Temple | 207 |
| Nehemiah asks the king for help | 211 |
| Repairing the city walls | 212 |
| Nehemiah the governor | 214 |
| Ezra reads God's laws to the people | 217 |
| Festival time | 218 |
| God promises a special king | 221 |

| | |
|---|---|
| Old and New Testament time chart | 222/223 |

| | |
|---|---|
| New Testament Contents | 224 |

# THE OLD TESTAMENT

## IN THE BEGINNING

### The Creation

In the beginning everything was dark. There was no world at all, only emptiness, but God was there and he was not dark or empty.

God said, 'Let there be light!' And there was light. Now life could begin.

So God shaped the world; he made the sky, the land and the sea. The earth was hot. Fire rumbled in the heart of the mountains. They exploded.

Then, slowly, the earth cooled, leaving rich soil where plants could grow. God was pleased with the world he had made.

4

Now he wanted plants to grow on the earth. Green shoots sprang up, and flowers opened their gay petals. Grass spread over the hills and valleys and a gentle wind rustled the leaves of countless trees. God saw that it was all good.

The green shoots grew tall and yellow. Grain ripened in the sun, but no little harvest mice ran through the corn. No birds nested in the tall trees. No children played yet in the new world.

So God spoke to the sea and the sky, 'Be filled with living things, too!' Fish of every shape and colour filled the sea. In the sky above, birds flew, soaring high as they sang. Insects hovered over the earth. Then God said, 'Let the earth be filled with animals of every kind!' Large animals roamed over the earth, and small ones scuttled after them. The air was filled with roars, neighs and squeals. God blessed them. Their numbers grew. God was pleased with everything he had made.

Now the earth was ready for people to live on it. God took a handful of soil and made a man. He breathed his life-giving breath into him. The man was different from all the other animals God made.

'I have made you like myself,' said God. 'You can understand the beauty of the world around you. You can speak. You can love.' The man opened his eyes and looked with wonder at the world God had made.

God went on, 'All this new world is for you. I have given you all you need. You can pick fruit to eat, and drink the water from the rivers and streams which flow over the land. Use this new world well.'

## The Garden of Eden

God placed the man in a beautiful garden called Eden. The man wandered through it, looking at the flowers which were so

beautiful that he reached out his hands to touch them. Sounds came to his ears; the glad songs of the birds, the buzzing of insects and the chatter of running water. The man caught some water in his cupped hands. He drank. He felt hungry and picked some fruit; it tasted sweet and juicy on his tongue. Everything was good.

The man was happy in the garden, and best of all, God talked to him. 'Look after my garden,' he told the man. 'Eat as much fruit as you like from any of the trees, but there is one tree in the middle of the garden whose fruit you must not eat. It would make you understand bad things as well as good. You will die on the day you eat it!'

Then God said, 'It's not good for the man to be alone,' and he brought the animals and birds to him to keep him company.

The man gave them each a name. He called the powerful beast with huge paws 'lion'. The woolly, new-born frisky one he called 'lamb'.

He named the lumbering elephant and the swift deer. He named the tiger and the ladybird, the eagle and the sparrow.

The man played with his new friends until he began to feel drowsy. He lay down and fell asleep.

Then God thought, 'Although the man can play with the animals, and they can help him in the garden, he has no real friend and partner to share things with.'

So while the man was still sleeping deeply, God made a woman. When the man woke up she was by his side.

'Now I am truly happy! You have given me the partner I need, and I am complete!' the man exclaimed joyfully to God. And he took the woman in his arms.

## The cunning snake

The man and his wife lived happily together in the garden. They wore no clothes but it did not matter to them. Together they worked, tending the plants, pruning the trees where the branches grew too thickly, digging the rich soil for the new seeds to grow, and picking fruit for their food.

Whenever they felt tired they rested in the shade or bathed in the river that ran through Eden.

Whenever they felt hungry they ate. In the evenings, when the garden was quiet and cool, the Lord God walked among the trees.

Whenever he called them the man and woman would run to him, drawn by the sound of his voice.

The man and woman loved each other and never spoke angrily or quarrelled. Then, one day the woman went off by herself through the flowers.

As she wandered she heard a rustle among the leaves of a nearby tree. A long snake was coiled round its trunk. Now the snake was the most cunning creature of all, and to the woman's surprise it began to question her.

'Is it true that God really told you not to eat any of the fruit in the garden?'

'Not at all!' the woman answered. 'We may eat as much fruit as we like, except from one tree. God warned us that we should die on the day we eat its fruit.'

'Surely God hasn't said so?' hissed the snake. 'See, you have found this delicious fruit of which God spoke, the fruit that makes you wise. Eat! You will understand everything, just like God!'

The woman looked at the tree and saw that its branches were indeed bowed beneath the weight of shining fruit, which looked so delicious she longed to taste some.

'How wonderful to be wise!' sighed the woman, tricked by the snake, and she picked some fruit and began to eat it slowly. At that moment her husband came up.

'You're eating the forbidden fruit!' he cried. 'You'll die!'

'I have eaten and have not died,' laughed the woman. 'The fruit has given me wisdom. It is the sweetest in the garden. Taste it and see.'

So the man took some fruit and ate it, too. At once he and the woman looked at each other with a new understanding.

'We are naked!' they realised, and now they felt ashamed. They tore down thick leaves from the fig tree and sewed them together to make clothing.

### A friendship spoilt

That evening they heard God calling them as he walked in the garden and they felt a new thing, fear. They had broken the only rule in the garden and they hid, afraid.

'Where are you?' God called. 'Why are you hiding?' The man and the woman crept out to meet him, but their friendship with God was spoilt.

'I was afraid because I was naked and so I hid,' the man lied.

'How did you know you were naked?' asked God. 'Have you been eating the fruit I said you were not to eat?'

'It was the woman,' the man blamed his wife. 'She gave it to me.'

'Why did you eat the fruit?' God asked the woman.

'The snake tricked me,' she replied.

guarding the gates with a sword of fire so that they could never return.

They knew that one day their bodies would die, but already the fresh loveliness they knew in God's perfect world had died for them, because they had disobeyed God's rule and eaten the fruit that would make them wise.

'Evil has come into my garden,' said God. 'Do you hear me, snake? From now on this woman's children will be your enemies, and you will go crawling along the ground.'

Then God turned to the woman. 'Because you listened to the snake, you will give birth to your babies in pain, and know longing and sorrow in your marriage.

'As for you, man, you have had an easy life here. The ground gave you good crops which you harvested easily. From now on you will sweat to get your food.'

Then God made clothing out of animal skins for the man and the woman and sent them away from Eden for ever. Sadly they wandered away from the garden. Behind them, an angel stood

# SAFE IN THE ARK

## Cain and Abel

The man and the woman settled down together in the world outside the Garden of Eden. They worked hard to get their food, just as God had said they would have to do. They often felt tired and hungry, but now they knew that if they stopped working there would be no food for them to eat.

Often they quarrelled. It was very different from the happy life they had led in Eden. But although they had spoilt their friendship with God, he still loved them, and he still looked after them, though they did not always realise it.

After a while the woman became pregnant and had a baby son. The man and the woman had names now; the man called his wife Eve, and she called him Adam.

They decided to give their son a name, too, and they called him Cain. Later on they had another son, and they called him Abel.

As they grew up, the two boys had to help their parents with the work. Cain used to grow vegetables and wheat, while Abel looked after the flocks of sheep and goats. Because of the evil that had come into the world when Adam and Eve disobeyed God, they were not a happy family. Cain was often jealous of Abel, and sometimes hated him secretly.

One day when they were both grown up, they decided to give God a present. They built a mound of stones to put their presents on. Then Cain brought some of his vegetables and grain, and Abel brought a lamb, carefully choosing the best of his flock.

God was more pleased with Abel's present than with Cain's because Abel had given the best he had. Cain noticed this and scowled angrily.

'Don't look so angry,' God warned Cain. 'Bad temper can make you hurt other people; it will get the better of you if you let it.'

Cain was too jealous and angry to listen. 'Come into the fields,' he told Abel, and there he killed his brother.

At once he heard God ask, 'Where is your brother?'

'How should I know?' replied Cain.

'Why have you done this dreadful thing? You have murdered your brother,' said God. 'Now you must leave this place. You can no longer grow your crops in the soil where your brother lies dead!'

So Cain had to go away from his sad parents, but God still looked after him wherever he went. At last he settled in a distant land where he built a city and raised a family of his own.

## Noah builds a boat

Many hundreds of years went by. The world began to fill with people, but they were wicked. They robbed and killed each other until God felt sorry that he had ever made human beings who treated one another so badly.

He was angry at the wrong he saw. At last there was only one man left who still loved God and followed his ways. His name was Noah.

So God warned Noah, 'People are so cruel that they are destroying one another and my beautiful world. I am going to send lots of rain. All the lakes and rivers, even the sea itself, will overflow and rush over the earth, until every living thing has been drowned in the flood.

'I promise I shall keep you and your family safe,' God continued. 'You must build a boat...'

God told Noah exactly how the boat was to be made. It was to be built of a special kind of wood and was to have three decks. The whole boat was to be 150 metres long and it was to be coated inside and outside with tar to make it watertight.

Noah obeyed God's instructions down to the smallest detail. His whole family helped him.

Every day astonished crowds watched them as they cut down trees and smoothed the wood. Slowly the boat began to take shape, but the bystanders jeered. 'Noah is mad,' they said. 'There is no water here to float a ship!'

Noah took not the slightest notice. Then God told him to drive into the boat two of every kind of animal, bird and reptile.

So Noah and his family rounded up the animals and drove them in. Two by two, one male and one female – tigers, elephants,

sparrows and mice, all had to be aboard before the rain came.

When the animals were safely settled in the boat Noah and his family went aboard, too. They took a last look at the old world. Then God himself shut the door behind them.

### The flood

There was a flash of lightning and a crash of thunder. The dark swollen clouds that filled the sky burst and it began to rain. Water poured down the hills and, filling the valleys, rose higher and higher.

The big boat jolted and began to drift, gently floating on the flood.

Everywhere people tried to escape. Faster and faster rose the boat on the foaming swirling water until it was tossed high above the tops of the highest mountains.

Every living thing on earth drowned as the sea covered the whole world.

Inside, Noah and his company were crowded and a bit cramped. The family was busy from morning until night cleaning the pens, changing the straw, bringing food and water to the animals.

They looked after them all, especially the ones that were seasick, and they even found time to play with their new friends.

For forty days and forty nights the sound of rain continued overhead. But God did not forget Noah and the animals in the boat. At last the rain died away and a wind blew over the flooded world. Slowly the water went down until at last the boat came to rest on the top of a double-peaked mountain called Ararat.

The wind kept blowing. Soon the peaks of other mountains showed like rocks sticking out of the sea.

Noah opened a trap-door and looked about. He decided to send a raven out to investigate. The bird gave a harsh croak and flew away. It never came back to the boat, but circled the flooded country looking for somewhere to rest. So a little later Noah sent out a dove.

Everyone gathered round to watch as the bird shook its white feathers and flew off, but it found nowhere to settle and came back to the boat. A week later Noah tried again. All day the family watched anxiously. Then in the evening the bird came back. Everyone cheered when they saw that the bird held an olive leaf in its beak. Now they knew the trees were beginning to grow. Soon they would be able to leave their boat and make a fresh start in God's new world.

At last the day came when God said to Noah, 'You may let the animals out now.' With a flurry of feathers and a pounding of hooves they rushed out of the boat, and raced away to find new homes.

Last of all Noah and his family stepped shakily off the boat, taking gulps of fresh air and stretching arms and legs. It was good to be alive in this clean new world.

As a way of saying thank you to God for this fresh start, Noah built a mound of stones and offered some birds and animals to him.

Then God said to Noah, 'I will never send another flood to destroy the world. Until the end of time there will always be times to plant and times to harvest, hot weather and cold weather, day and night.'

God told Noah and his family and all the living things about this promise.

'Look, I am putting my bow in the sky so that you will remember my promise. When the rainbow shines against stormy clouds you will know that I am reminding you that I shall never again send a flood to destroy the earth.'

A wonderful coloured arc glowed in the sky. Noah and his family went singing on their way under the rainbow.

# ABRAHAM'S FAMILY

## *Abraham goes on a long journey*

Noah and his family worked hard in the new world. They farmed the land to grow food for themselves. When Noah's grandchildren grew up, they moved to other countries and built cities. After hundreds of years the world was full of people again. They began to discover new ways of doing things — they built stronger houses and made fine clothes. Different groups began to speak in different ways, and new languages grew up. Everybody was so busy that they began to forget what they knew about God.

At last there was no one left who really knew what God was like. People worshipped different gods, the sun and moon and figures made of stone. God knew that he must start teaching people about himself again.

In the city of Haran, in the country we now call Turkey, lived a man named Abraham. The people of Haran were wealthy. They built stone houses round shady courtyards to keep them cool in the hot sun. Their houses were filled with beautiful furniture and pottery, and they wore fine clothes and jewels.

One day Abraham stood watching as a large crowd went singing and dancing down the street. They were on their way to worship the moon god.

'Why should I join the others?' Abraham said to himself. 'They are going to worship the moon – I want to worship the God who made the moon and the sun.'

Then God spoke to Abraham, 'You must leave Haran and go to a new country which I will show you. I will lead you there and give the country to you and your children. You will become the father of a great nation.'

Abraham did as God had told him. He and his wife Sarah and their nephew, Lot, left their comfortable life in the city and set off to find the unknown country God had promised them. They lived in tents which they carried with them. They took flocks of sheep and goats to give them milk and food on the journey. Servants and herdsmen travelled with them to look after the animals.

They travelled slowly, camping wherever they found water and moving on again. Lot had sheep of his own and tents and servants, too. But the rough, hilly country provided poor grazing for so many flocks. Sometimes there wasn't enough room to pitch all the tents around the wells where they camped. Trouble started, for Lot's servants began to fight with Abraham's men.

'We must part company,' said Abraham to Lot. 'The whole land lies before us. You choose which way you want to go, and I will take the opposite direction.'

Lot chose the best-looking land that lay in the rich, fertile plain of the Jordan. He and his men set out and camped near a city called Sodom where the people were cruel and wicked and no one worshipped God.

True to his promise, Abraham and his men went the opposite way and pitched their tents in the land of Canaan. Then God spoke to Abraham again. 'Look around you, Abraham. Look north, south, east and west. This is the land I promised you. It will belong to you and to your children's children for ever. I will give it to you.

I will make such a great nation come from you that no one will be able to count them all. If anyone ever managed to count every single speck of dust on the ground, only then would they know the number of your descendants.'

Although Abraham and Sarah still had no children, and Sarah was growing old, Abraham believed God's promise. He built an altar of stones, lit a fire on it and worshipped God.

One day a messenger brought bad news to Abraham. Lot was a prisoner. 'Our enemies made war on Sodom and four of the other cities in the plain where Lot lives,' said the messenger. 'The kings of Sodom and the other cities called out their armies and marched across the valley to fight their attackers. The battle went against them and the king of Sodom tried to run away, but he stumbled into a deep tar pit. Then the enemy took everyone in Sodom prisoner, including your nephew, Lot, and seized all our possessions. I got away and came to tell you.'

Abraham gathered the warriors from his followers. They chased after the enemy. When darkness came they made a surprise attack and rescued Lot and his family and possessions. Then they drove the defeated armies far away to the north.

### God's promise comes true

Many years went by. God repeated his promise to give Abraham and Sarah many descendants, but still they had no child.

One afternoon Abraham was sitting in the shade of his tent. It was the hottest time of day. Suddenly he saw three strangers approaching. Abraham ran up to them and bowed to the ground.

'Welcome, sirs,' he said. 'Please stop here to rest. Let me send for water so that you may wash your feet. If you will sit down in the shade of these trees, I will go and prepare food for you.'

'Thank you,' the strangers replied and Abraham hurried back to his tent. He called Sarah, and they prepared for the strangers a feast of meal and cakes and veal, butter and milk. Abraham took the food to the strangers.

'Where is your wife, Sarah?' they asked.

'She is close by − in the tent.'

'Next year,' they said, 'God will give Sarah a son!'

Sarah overheard the conversation and laughed to herself. 'I'm too old to have a baby now,' she thought.

But she was wrong. Next year she had a baby boy, just as the strangers said. Because she had laughed at the idea she called the baby 'Isaac', which means 'laughter'.

Their baby made them very happy, and Isaac grew up into a strong young boy.

God was pleased that Abraham had trusted him to give them a son. Now he decided to see if Abraham still trusted him and wanted to obey him.

'Take your son, Isaac,' said God, 'and offer him as a sacrifice to me.' Abraham was broken-hearted at the thought of sacrificing his son, but he still trusted God, and wanted to do what God told him. Early one

morning before anyone else was awake, Abraham called two of his servants to prepare for a journey. Then he woke Isaac. Together the four of them set out for a high mountain, three days' journey from their camp.

Here Abraham told the servants to wait. 'Isaac and I will go up the mountain to pray,' he said. Abraham had brought firewood from home which he gave to Isaac to carry. 'Are we going to burn a sacrifice?' Isaac asked.

'Yes,' replied his father.

'Where is the animal for our sacrifice?' panted Isaac as they climbed up the steep mountain.

'God will provide it, Isaac,' answered Abraham.

Isaac looked around, but there was no sign of a goat or a lamb anywhere on the hillside.

After a time they reached a rocky place where thorn bushes grew. Abraham stopped and untied Isaac's load of firewood. He made an altar and piled the wood on top.

Then Abraham picked Isaac up. He tied him to the altar and raised his knife.

'Abraham! Abraham! Don't harm your son!' came God's voice. 'Now I know that you trust me and love me with all your heart because you were ready to offer your only son to me.'

Abraham looked up. As he did so he saw a stray ram caught in a thorn bush by its long curling horns.

'God has provided our sacrifice,' Abraham exclaimed joyfully. He untied Isaac and hugged him close. Then he offered the ram on the altar instead of his son. As the flames leapt upwards God spoke to Abraham again.

'Because you were ready to give up your son to me, I promise that I will give you as many descendants as there are stars in the sky or grains of sand along the seashore.'

Abraham and Isaac worshipped God, and then Abraham took his son home. Now he knew for sure that God would never fail him.

## Rebekah and Isaac

By the time Isaac was grown up, Abraham was a very old man and Sarah had died. Abraham decided it was time for Isaac to marry and have children of his own. He sent a servant all the way back to Haran. 'I'm sure some of my family will still be living in Haran,' Abraham explained to his servant. 'I want you to find them and choose a bride for Isaac from among the young girls, as our custom is.'

The servant set out on his journey. He took some of the other servants with him and a string of camels laden with expensive presents for the bride.

'How will I find the right girl when I get to Haran?' the servant puzzled.

At last the walls of Haran came in sight. The servant got off his camel and waited beside the well.

He began to pray, 'Please help me to find my master's family in this foreign place.'

Just then he heard talking and laughter. 'The girls are coming to fetch water from the well,' he thought. Then he had an idea and prayed again. 'Lord, I'll ask one of the girls for a drink. If she gives me a drink from her jar and offers to give my camels water, too, let her be the bride you've chosen for my master's son.'

A girl came up to the well before he had finished his prayer.

'Please give me a drink,' the servant said.

She held her heavy water jar out at once. 'Of course. I'll fill the water trough for your camels, too,' she said and ran back to the well. She emptied jar after jar into the trough and the thirsty camels crowded round greedily while the servant watched in wonder because God had answered his prayer so quickly.

When the camels had drunk enough the servant gave the girl two heavy gold bracelets and a ring.

'What's your name?' he asked.

'Rebekah,' she replied. 'My family all live in Haran but my father's brother whose name is Abraham left home and moved to Canaan.'

As soon as the servant heard this he bowed down to the ground and thanked God that he had found his master's relations so soon.

Rebekah hurried home to tell everyone her story. Her family welcomed the servant and gave him a good meal. Then the servant asked them if Rebekah could go back to Canaan with him and marry Isaac.

'You must ask Rebekah herself,' they said.

'Yes, I'll go with you and marry Isaac,' Rebekah agreed.

She got herself ready and set off with Abraham's servant. They rode on their camels for many miles until one evening as they passed through the quiet fields a man came hurrying to meet them.

'Who's that?' Rebekah asked the servant.

'It's Isaac, my master's son,' he replied.

Rebekah hid her face in her veil and slid down from her camel as Isaac ran up to her. He fell in love with her at once and took her to meet Abraham in his tent. So Rebekah became Isaac's bride and found a new home in Abraham's family.

## Jacob and Esau

Rebekah and Isaac were very happy together except that they had no children. So Isaac asked God for a child, and in time Rebekah had twin sons. They called the boys Esau and Jacob.

The twins were very different. Jacob was his mother's favourite. He stayed at home and minded the sheep and goats, but Esau grew up to be a strong red-headed man who liked to go hunting. His father enjoyed the tasty venison he brought home for the pot. Esau was his favourite son!

By now Abraham was dead and Isaac himself was an old man. Jacob knew that when Isaac died, Esau, who was the elder of the twins, would own most of their father's wealth and rule over the family.

One day Esau came home tired out and very hungry. Jacob was cooking lentils in a big pot.

'I'm starving! Give me some of that stew you're cooking before I die on my feet!' Esau begged him.

Jacob stirred the thick red stew thoughtfully. 'All right, you can have some,' he said, 'but only if you agree to give me your rights, as the eldest, to our father's goods!'

'What good will they be to me if I die of hunger?' cried Esau. 'You can have them!'

'Promise,' insisted Jacob. 'Otherwise you'll forget our agreement when you're feeling full!' So Esau promised and gobbled down the stew which Jacob gave him. 'Is that all he cares about being the eldest?' thought Jacob.

### Jacob steals the blessing

Isaac was now so old that he could no longer see clearly, but he still loved the taste of good meat. 'My son,' he said to Esau one day, 'if you go hunting and catch me a tasty dinner I will give you my special blessing. Then your life will be rich and happy and you will rule over your brother Jacob. No one will be able to take my blessing from you.'

Rebekah overheard. Quickly she hurried to find Jacob. 'Go to your flock of goats,' she said, 'and fetch me two good kids. We'll make your father a savoury stew of the kind he likes, before Esau returns from his hunting. Then you can take it to your father. He will eat it, and bless you, because he'll think you are Esau.'

While Rebekah made the stew she told Jacob to dress up in

Esau's clothes. She even draped goat-skins round his neck and over his hands so that he would feel as hairy as his twin.

When everything was prepared, Jacob took the stew to his father.

'Which of my sons is it?' asked Isaac.

'Esau,' lied Jacob.

'Let me feel you,' said Isaac. He ran his shaky hands over Jacob's face and wrists. 'He has Jacob's voice, but Esau's smell and feel,' he murmured to himself. 'Are you really Esau?'

'Yes,' lied Jacob again. So Isaac ate the stew, and gave Jacob his special blessing, which would make him more important than his brother. Satisfied, Jacob hurried away.

A little later Esau came hurrying in carrying his bowl of stew. 'Here it is, Father. Eat it and bless me!' he called.

Isaac trembled with dismay. 'I have already blessed a man with Jacob's voice, but Esau's smell and feel. I can't bless you, too!'

'That was Jacob!' shouted Esau angrily. 'He cheated me out of my share of your goods, and now he's stolen my blessing!'

Esau was furious, for a blessing was like an arrow in flight. It couldn't be recalled. From then on he hated Jacob and threatened to kill him. Jacob had to run away, and Rebekah sent him to her brother Laban in Haran for safety.

## Jacob's dream

The road to Haran lay across desolate countryside. Jacob travelled alone with only a strong stick to protect him from wild animals and robbers. At night he slept on his thick sheepskin coat with a stone for a pillow.

One night he had a dream. He saw a ladder with hundreds of steps stretching from earth to heaven. Bright angels crowded up and down it. Then he heard God's voice telling him that one day he would return safely to his own country.

Jacob woke up. 'The Lord is in this place, and I didn't know it,' he exclaimed. Next morning, as a gift for God, he poured precious olive oil over the stone he had used as a pillow. 'If you keep me safe and provide for me I shall worship you as my God,' he promised. Then he went on his way. God was with him and led him safely to his uncle, Laban.

On his way Jacob met a pretty shepherd girl called Rachel.

'That's Laban's daughter,' some other shepherds said. 'She's bringing her sheep here for water.' Jacob ran off at once to help her. He rolled back the heavy stone which covered the well and poured out water for the sheep to drink. When the shepherd girl tried to thank him, he laughed and kissed her.

'I'm your cousin,' he explained, but he didn't tell her that he had fallen in love with her!

Rachel ran home to tell her father who gave Jacob a great welcome. Jacob met the rest of the family, including Rachel's big sister Leah. He stayed a whole month with them and worked hard, helping his uncle with the sheep.

'You shouldn't do all this work for me without any payment, just because you're a nephew of mine,' Laban said. 'What shall I pay you for helping me?'

'I'll work for seven years more for you if only you'll let me marry Rachel!' Jacob said at once.

'Of course,' Laban agreed and so Jacob stayed for seven years and worked hard for Laban. He loved Rachel so much that the time passed very quickly. He watched her grow up and each year she seemed more beautiful than ever.

## Laban cheats Jacob

When seven years had gone by Jacob reminded Laban of his promise and Laban prepared a wedding feast and invited all his friends and neighbours, but Rachel's sister, Leah, was nowhere to be seen. Of course, as the custom was, the bride herself was wrapped in veils.

Next morning Jacob pulled back the curtains and saw the face of the girl who slept beside him. It was Leah.

Jacob jumped up and rushed off to find Laban. 'You've cheated me,' he complained. 'I worked seven years for Rachel and you've married me off to Leah. Why have you tricked me?'

Laban tried to soothe his angry nephew. 'Didn't you know that the custom of our country is that the elder girl must marry first?' he explained. 'I couldn't let you marry Rachel, but listen, just wait till all the festivities are over and the guests have gone home and I shall give you Rachel, too, providing you work for another seven years for me.'

Jacob had to agree. There was nothing he could do. He had no possessions except the rights to his father's goods he had stolen from his brother and the blessing that he had tricked his father into giving him.

At the end of the week Rachel became his wife. Jacob paid little attention to Leah now that Rachel was his, but over the years Leah had four boys in a row and Rachel didn't have any children at all.

In the end Rachel did have a son, and Jacob loved him best of all his children. He called him Joseph.

### The brothers make friends again

Jacob stayed a long time with Laban. He worked hard and became quite rich. He had lots of sheep and goats and had fathered eleven sons and daughters. Everyone could see that God was looking after him, but Jacob was still scared of his brother Esau.

At last God told Jacob it was time for him to go back to his own country and, although Jacob was afraid, he did what God said.

When they were nearly home they heard that Esau was coming to meet them with four hundred men. Jacob was terrified but he prayed that God would keep his family safe. When Esau came into sight, Jacob bowed to the ground in front of his brother, but Esau

lifted him up and hugged him. So Jacob introduced Esau to his whole family and gave him presents from his flocks. 'Do take them,' he urged. 'God has been good to me, and has given me everything I need, but best of all he has made us friends again.'

So the brothers parted in peace and Jacob and his family travelled on. But before they had gone much further something very sad happened. Rachel died giving birth to her second son.

They buried Rachel in a town called Bethlehem. Sadly Jacob travelled on. He called his new baby Benjamin. He loved Joseph more than ever now that Rachel had died and always favoured him more than the other boys.

# JOSEPH

### *The favourite son*

One day when Joseph was quite big, Jacob gave his favourite son a beautiful long-sleeved coat. His brothers were jealous.

They were very angry and couldn't say a kind word to Joseph.

They were even angrier when Joseph told them about the dreams he had. 'I dreamt we were all in the fields at harvest time,' he told them. 'We were tying up the sheaves. My sheaf stood up and yours all came and bowed down to it.'

'You're too big for your boots!' they snarled. 'You strut around in your fine new coat and think you can boss us about.'

'Well my next dream's even better! The sun and moon and eleven stars came and bowed down to me!'

The brothers knew that Joseph thought they were the eleven stars, and his mother and father were the moon and the sun. They were furious. Even Jacob scolded him when he overheard him telling his dream, but the old man often thought about his son's dreams and wondered whether they would come true.

Some time afterwards, Joseph's ten older brothers took their father's flocks of sheep and goats to new pastures. Jacob sent Joseph along after them to take them food and see how they were.

Joseph put on his fine new coat and set off. His brothers saw him in the distance. 'Look! Here comes the dreamer!' they cried. 'Let's tear his coat off him and kill him. We'll tell our father a wild animal ate up his dear little Joseph!'

But the eldest brother, Reuben, said, 'No, we want no bloodshed.

Don't kill the boy, just teach him a lesson – he certainly needs one – but don't let's hurt him. Throw him in this empty well here.' The others agreed.

'Hello there, brothers,' called out Joseph, never guessing what danger he was in.

'I've walked a long way with all this food for you.'

They crowded around Joseph, tugging at his new coat.

'Hey, stop it! Leave me alone! Father said...' Joseph began.

'Father's a long way away at home!' they sneered.

They tore off Joseph's coat, beat him up and pushed him down the empty well. Then they sat down and were just about to enjoy the food Joseph had brought when they saw a line of camels coming slowly towards them.

'Traders on their way to Egypt!' they exclaimed. They hauled Joseph out of the well and, in spite of his protests, they sold him to the merchants for twenty silver coins. Joseph was tied up and led off to become a slave in Egypt.

The brothers killed a goat and dipped Joseph's coat in its blood. They took it home and showed it to Jacob. 'Look what we've found. Do you recognise it?' they asked.

'It's my son's coat,' cried the old man. 'Some wild animal must have eaten him.' He tore his clothes and no one could comfort him.

### Joseph the slave

Meanwhile, far away in Egypt, the Midianite traders put Joseph up for sale in a slave market. An Egyptian liked the look of him, and bought him. This man's name was Potiphar. He was an officer in the king of Egypt's guard.

At first everything went well for Joseph. His master was so pleased with him that he put him in charge of all his affairs.

'Your God gives you success in all you do,' he said. 'With you in charge I don't have any worries at all!'

But before long things grew difficult for Joseph. Potiphar's wife noticed her husband's handsome young slave and fell in love with him.

When Joseph refused to take any notice of her because she was his master's wife, she was furious. She told her husband lies about Joseph.

'Your slave has attacked me,' she claimed. 'I screamed, and he ran off, leaving his cloak behind.' Potiphar believed her.

He had Joseph arrested and thrown into prison.

### Joseph in prison

It was a terrible time for Joseph. He had no friends to visit him or to go to Potiphar to beg him to set him free. But God was still taking care of him. The chief jailer noticed him and was kind to him. Soon he had put Joseph in charge of other prisoners.

Some time later, Pharaoh, king of Egypt, was angry with two of his servants, his cupbearer and his chief baker. He had them put in the same prison as Joseph. One morning Joseph noticed they were looking worried, and when he asked them what was wrong they told him about the strange dreams they had had the night before.

'I saw a vine with three blossoming branches,' said the cupbearer. 'Grapes grew on the

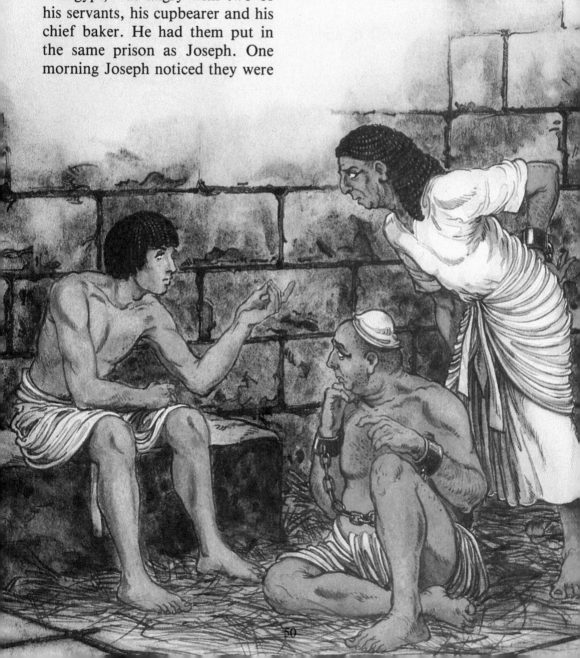

vine, and I squeezed their juice into Pharaoh's wine cup.'

'That's good,' said Joseph. 'The three branches mean three days. In three days you will get your old job back.'

'Let's hope my dream's a good one, too!' said the baker, cheering up. 'I was carrying three trays of cakes on my head. All Pharaoh's favourites were on top, but the birds flew down and ate them up.'

'I'm afraid that's bad,' said Joseph. 'Three trays are three days so you'll be hanged in three days and the birds will peck your bones.'

Three days later it was Pharaoh's birthday. He set the cupbearer free and gave him back his job, but the baker was hanged just as Joseph had said.

Joseph thought that perhaps if Pharaoh knew what had really happened to him he would be set free too. He asked the cupbearer to tell the king, but the man forgot.

### Pharaoh's strange dreams

Two whole years went by, and then Pharaoh himself had some strange dreams. He asked his wise men to explain them.

'I was standing on the banks of the River Nile. Seven fine fat cows came out of the water and started to graze among the rushes. Seven more cows followed but they were all skin and bones. Then a strange thing happened – the skinny cows ate the fat ones up.'

The wise men muttered together, but no one could tell the meaning of the dream.

'This is my second dream,' said Pharaoh. 'Seven fat ears of corn grew on one stalk. Then seven thin shrivelled ears of wheat sprouted and swallowed the good grain.' No one knew the meaning of the second dream either. Suddenly the cupbearer remembered Joseph. He whispered to his master the story of how Joseph had explained his and the baker's dreams when they were in prison. Pharaoh ordered his attendants to bring Joseph to him at once.

So Joseph came and stood before the king.

'Both dreams have the same meaning,' said Joseph when he heard Pharaoh's story. 'The seven fat cows and the seven fat ears of corn are seven years of plenty, of good harvests when all the barns in Egypt will be piled high with grain, and everyone will have more than enough to eat. The seven thin cows and the seven shrivelled ears of corn are years, too. They will follow the seven years of plenty, and they will be bad years when the harvest will be so poor that everyone will be hungry. This dream comes from God, and he has given you two dreams to show you that all this is definitely going to happen soon. Make plans now, and no one will die of hunger.'

'What should I do?' asked Pharaoh, impressed.

'You must collect a fifth of the harvest every year during the good years. Store it up in barns, and then, when the hungry times come, there will be food for everyone. Choose someone you can trust to organise it for you,' advised Joseph.

'A good idea!' approved Pharaoh. 'And you're the very man for the job!'

Then without delay Pharaoh hung a gold chain round Joseph's neck and put his own ring on his finger.

'Now you're the most important man in Egypt after me,' he said. 'Everyone will make way for you and do what you say.'

### Joseph and his brothers

So for seven years Joseph travelled up and down the land telling people to build storage towers and to fill them with grain ready for the bad years ahead.

When the bad years came, Joseph opened the stores so that the people could buy grain to make bread.

The harvest was bad in other countries, too. Far away, hungry people heard that there was corn for sale in Egypt.

When Jacob heard, he sent his sons all the way from Canaan to buy grain. Only the youngest, Benjamin, stayed at home; Jacob didn't want him to disappear as Joseph had done.

The brothers found the official in charge of the grain and bowed to the ground in front of him. They never guessed he was their long-lost brother, but Joseph recognised them and remembered his dreams long ago. He wondered whether his brothers had changed. Quickly he made a plan to test them.

'You're spies,' he challenged them. 'I'm not selling you any grain!'

'No, my lord. We are honest men, all brothers. Our youngest brother stayed at home with our old father Jacob, who sent us to buy grain for our families.'

'Bring your brother here and I'll know whether you're speaking the truth or not!' Joseph ordered. He made Simeon stay behind as a hostage, but gave the others grain.

'We're being punished now for the dreadful thing we did to Joseph,' the brothers said. Joseph was very upset, but pretended not to listen.

That night when the brothers were on the way home, one of them opened his sack and found on the top of the grain the money he had paid. To their dismay the others found their money had been returned, too.

'The governor will say we're thieves as well as spies. He'll think we took his grain without paying

the famine was so bad that they soon had to plan another journey to Egypt for corn.

'You must let Benjamin come with us this time, Father. That man will never give us any corn if we don't bring him along,' they argued, and Jacob finally gave way.

'Take the man a present of honey, nuts and spices – the best we've got. And give him back his money. It may have been a mistake,' Jacob advised.

So the brothers set off again with Benjamin.

When Joseph saw them coming he told his servants to invite them into his house for a meal. The brothers tried to return the money to Joseph's steward.

'Keep it,' he said. 'I was paid in full for all the corn you bought.'

He gave orders for Simeon to be brought out to them. Together again, but completely bewildered, the brothers waited for Joseph to arrive. When he came in, they bowed down before him and gave him their presents.

'Is your father well?' asked Joseph. 'Is this the brother you told me about? What a fine young man...' Joseph began, but the sight of his young brother made him so upset he had to rush out of the room before anyone noticed he was crying. Then he gave them a splendid meal and offered Benjamin five times as much food as anyone else.

for it. Whatever will happen when we go back?' they wondered.

When Jacob heard all this he was more determined than ever to keep Benjamin safely at home, but

Then, loaded with grain, the brothers set off for home. Surely nothing could go wrong now. Suddenly they heard the sound of galloping hooves, and they were overtaken by Joseph's steward, 'Stop thief!' he shouted. 'One of you has stolen my master's silver cup.'

They all looked anxiously on as sack after sack was opened. Then to their horror, 'There it is!' exclaimed the steward, pointing to Benjamin's sack. 'You'll be punished for this!' Miserably they all went back with him to the governor's house.

'The thief must stay here as my slave,' Joseph said.

All the brothers were filled with dismay. 'My father will die of a broken heart if Benjamin doesn't come home,' said Judah, one of the eleven brothers. 'Make me your slave instead, sir,' he begged.

Then Joseph saw that his brothers had changed and were no longer so cruel and jealous. Again he could hardly hide his tears. He

sent his servants away, and then he stopped pretending.

'Brothers, I am Joseph,' he told them, but they were too amazed and frightened to answer him.

'Don't be afraid,' he went on. 'God has turned the wrong you did to good. He has used me to save the lives of many people. Go and bring my father here to Egypt so that I can look after him.'

As soon as Pharaoh heard the news he offered land in Egypt to Joseph's father and brothers where they could settle with their families.

When old Jacob arrived in Egypt, Joseph rode out in his chariot to meet him. They flung their arms round each other and wept for joy.

'I can die happily for I have seen you again,' the old man said.

'Don't talk about dying, Father!' exclaimed Joseph. 'Look, now all our family is together again. God has been good to us!'

He led the way to Pharaoh's court where he could provide all that his family needed, and for many years afterwards they lived happily together in Egypt.

# MOSES THE PRINCE

### The baby in the basket

After Joseph and his brothers were dead their children and grandchildren still stayed in Egypt. When their great-great-grandchildren had grown up and were living in Egypt, the Egyptian rulers began to treat them badly. They made them work in slave gangs, building monuments and cities. This was bad enough, but finally one king gave an even crueller order – 'There are too many of these Hebrews', he said, calling them by the name that the Egyptians used. 'Throw all the baby Hebrew boys into the River Nile in case they grow up and fight us.'

One brave mother decided to hide her baby. When he was too big to hide in the house she daubed a basket with tar to make it watertight and put her son in it. Then she took the basket to the Nile and left it bobbing along the water among the tall papyrus reeds. The baby's older sister, Miriam, waited close by to see what would happen.

Before long one of the king's daughters came to bathe. She saw the basket and sent her maids to fetch it. The baby was crying and the princess felt sorry for him. She picked him up to comfort him.

Then Miriam came up and curtsied to the princess. 'Shall I find someone to look after him for you?' she asked, and, when the princess agreed, she ran and fetched her mother. 'I am adopting

this baby as my son,' the princess told the slave woman. 'If you look after him for me until he's bigger, I will pay you well.'

So the baby's mother took him home safely to look after him for the princess, and for some years the child grew up in his own family. His mother looked after him and taught him to worship the God of the Hebrew people. Then, when he was bigger, he went to live in the palace with the princess who gave him the name Moses.

## Moses runs away

One day, after he was quite grown up, Moses went to watch the Hebrew slaves, his own people, at work on a building site. He found them making bricks. As he watched he saw an Egyptian overseer beating a slave. Moses was angry. He glanced quickly this way and that, and when he thought no one was looking he killed the Egyptian and hid his body in the sand. The next day he went out again and met two Hebrews who were fighting. He tried to stop them. 'You shouldn't hit your fellow Hebrew,' he said.

'Who gave you the right to order us about?' snarled the slaves. 'Do you think you can kill us like you killed that Egyptian yesterday?' Moses was frightened to think that someone knew what he had done. If the king heard, he would be executed. He went back to the palace, but soon the king did hear and Moses had to run away to live

in the desert where no one would follow him. Only shepherds and their families lived there, wandering with their flocks wherever they could find water.

Before long Moses was in another fight. He was resting beside a well when seven girls, all sisters, the daughters of the priest of Midian, came along to fill their water jars. A crowd of shepherds came up and pushed the girls out of the way so that they could get to the water first. Moses leapt to his feet and drove the shepherds away. Then he helped the girls to fill their jars and give water to the flocks.

When the girls' father heard what he had done for them he was very pleased. He invited Moses to come and live with them in their tent and let him marry one of his daughters. So Moses settled in the desert and became a shepherd.

### Moses and the burning bush

Meanwhile, the other Hebrews were still slaves in Egypt. In their misery they called out to God to help them. God heard their prayers. It was time for his special people, the Hebrews, to be freed, and Moses was going to be part of God's rescue plan.

One day, as Moses led his father-in-law's flock across the desert he noticed that a bush had caught fire, but although flames crackled along the branches the bush wasn't burnt up. Moses went closer to see why. A voice called to him, 'Moses!' It seemed to be coming out of the fire.

'Here I am,' answered Moses.

'Don't come any closer! Take off your sandals! This is holy ground. I am God!' Moses hid his face in fear. He was even more frightened when he heard God say, 'I am sending you to the king of Egypt to rescue the Hebrew people from slavery.' He began to make excuses.

'No one will believe me. I'm just a nobody. I can't even speak properly. They'll never listen to me!'

'I will go with you,' God promised. 'When the Egyptian priests try their magic out on you, I'll help you to do even more wonderful things. I'll tell you what to say.'

'Please choose someone else,' Moses begged.

God grew angry. 'I have chosen you,' he said, 'but I shall send your brother Aaron to meet you. He will speak for you and I'll help you both.'

So Moses set off for Egypt.

His brother Aaron met him in the desert just as God had promised. The two brothers were delighted to be together again. Quickly they made their way to Egypt. At once Moses and Aaron gathered the Hebrew leaders together. Aaron told them how God had spoken to Moses from the burning bush.

When the Hebrews understood that God had sent Moses to rescue them, they knelt down, full of happiness, and worshipped God.

### Moses and Aaron go to see the king

Then Moses and Aaron went to see the king with their message. 'Our God says, "Let my people go away to the desert to pray to me there," ' they said.

'What nonsense!' exclaimed the king furiously. 'It's just an excuse to stop working.' He called his overseers. 'The Hebrew slaves must be made to work harder. They're lazy! You give them straw to make their bricks, don't you? Well from now on they must find their own straw and still make the same number of bricks!'

The slaves complained bitterly to Moses when they heard: 'See what you've done with your talk of freedom, you've only brought us worse trouble!'

So Moses prayed to God, and God said to him, 'The king of Egypt is stubborn, but the Egyptians will learn that I am God, because I am going to show them my power, and force them to let my people go.'

Then Moses and Aaron went back to the king.

'You must prove that your God is real if you want me to listen to you,' said the king. Aaron threw

covered with snakes – until Aaron's ate up the others! Still the king wasn't convinced and he refused to let the slaves go.

So God told Moses he would

his stick to the ground and it turned into a snake.

'That's an old trick,' jeered the king. He ordered his magicians to do the same. The floor was

show the king of Egypt even more of his power. Moses and Aaron went to meet the king by the River Nile.

'God sent me to tell you to let his

people go, but you wouldn't listen. Now look at the water, your Majesty.'

The king looked. The water had turned blood red. It stank. Dead fish swirled in the scum on the surface. All over Egypt the water in jugs and jars turned into blood, too. Desperately people began to dig along the river banks to find fresh water, but the king went back to the palace and paid no attention to Moses.

Then millions of frogs swarmed over Egypt. They hopped out of the Nile; and out of every pool and canal. They went everywhere, into the ovens and the cooking pots. They even found their way into the king's bedroom and hopped over his bed.

'Pray to your God for us!' the king begged Moses. 'Ask him to get rid of these frogs.'

Moses prayed and God answered his prayer. The frogs died. There were large piles of dead frogs everywhere, and the whole country stank of them. In spite of this the king still refused to let the Hebrews go. Now God sent swarms of mosquitoes which tormented everyone. Still the king took no notice. Flies attacked the crops. Cattle and camels died of disease, but the king would not let the slaves go.

### Disaster in Egypt

After the flies had gone, everyone in Egypt was covered with painful boils. Still the king would not listen to God. Even the court magicians could do nothing about them and they were covered with boils, too. However, it made no difference to the king; he still refused to let the slaves go.

'Warn the king that I am going to send such a heavy hailstorm that any animals or people left outside will die in it,' God told Moses.

Storm clouds blew up and thunder rumbled across the sky. Lightning struck the earth. Huge hailstones beat down all the plants and killed every living thing that was still outside.

'This is the worst storm Egypt has ever had, and it's all my fault,' groaned the king.

'Moses, pray that God will stop the hail, and I'll let you all go!'

'I'll pray,' said Moses quietly, 'but I know you won't keep your promise.'

Moses prayed. The storm stopped, and at once the king changed his mind and refused to let the slaves leave. So God punished Egypt again. He sent clouds of locusts to eat up all the plants that were still alive after the hail, so that nothing green was left on plant or tree. Then he sent a great darkness which covered the land for three days so that people couldn't see one another, but in spite of all this, the king refused to do what God wanted.

Then Moses called the Hebrews together and said, 'Because the king of Egypt won't listen to God, the eldest son in every family in Egypt is going to die! Your children will escape if you do as God says. Each family must kill a lamb and smear some of its blood over the door of their house. Then the death which God is sending will not touch your homes. And tonight you must be ready to leave, because this time the king will let us go!'

The Hebrews did as Moses told them. When they had smeared their doors with the blood they stood inside, dressed and ready for their journey, eating their supper and waiting for the order to move. At midnight they heard a sound of crying from the houses of the Egyptians. Every eldest son had died, the king's among them.

The king called for Moses and Aaron. 'Go and take your people with you,' he ordered, 'or else we shall all be dead.' He was very frightened.

None of the Egyptians wanted the Hebrews to stay. When the slaves asked their masters for gold and silver and clothing for the journey the Egyptians loaded them with treasure — they were so glad to be rid of the people who had brought them so much trouble.

### Escape from Egypt

So at last the Hebrews made their way out of Egypt and into the desert. There were no roads to follow, but God sent a great cloud like a billowing pillar ahead of them and they followed it each day. At night the cloud turned to fire, giving them light for their journey. The people were glad because they could see that God was with them, leading them on and looking after them.

The king wasn't going to let his slaves escape so easily, though! He felt sorry already that he had let them go. 'Chase them!' he ordered his soldiers. He jumped into his war chariot. Six hundred of his best charioteers, as well as the rest of his army, thundered after the Hebrews.

Soon the Hebrews heard the sound of the horsemen following them. They had reached the sea,

but they had no boats. They turned on Moses in terror.

'You should have left us in Egypt! We're trapped! The soldiers will cut us to pieces!' they cried, as the sound of hooves grew nearer.

'Don't be afraid. God will fight for us,' Moses encouraged them.

'Look!' someone pointed. 'The pillar of cloud has moved. It's

behind us now! It's hiding us from the army!'

'Stretch your hand out over the sea,' God told Moses. As he obeyed an easterly gale sprang up, pounding the sea and sweeping back the waves. A path appeared. Without wasting a minute, the Hebrews hurried across between the towering banks of water.

The Egyptians charged after them, but their chariots stuck fast in the wet mud. 'Stretch your hand over the sea again,' God said to Moses. 'The water will come back before the Egyptians can catch you.'

'Hurry!' Moses called to the people as they scrambled up the shore. He lifted his hand. The sea foamed back across the path, covering the Egyptian army. Not a soldier was left alive.

The Hebrews watched in amazement until suddenly Miriam, Moses' sister, shook her tambourine.

'Sing to our God who has won a great victory. Drowning the Egyptian army in the middle of the sea!'

The women joined her, singing and dancing, while the men laughed and stamped and the children swayed to the music.

'The sea stood up just like a wall. The Lord our God has saved us all,' they sang, forgetting their fear and their complaints.

In all the years to come they never forgot the wonderful way God had saved them from the Egyptians by leading them safely across the middle of the sea.

## MOSES AND JOSHUA

### Food in the desert

The Hebrew people still had a long way to journey to the new country God had promised to them. Soon they reached the desert where the earth was dry and hard underfoot. Nothing grew there but thorn bushes where jackals lurked. As the long line of people followed Moses they began to grumble and complain to him. 'Why did you take us away from Egypt? At least we had plenty to eat there! We'll starve to death here in the desert!'

'God rescued you from Egypt,' Moses reminded them. 'He has heard your complaints and he will give you food even out here. Why don't you trust him?'

Next morning the ground was covered with something thin and

flaky like frost. 'Gather it before it melts,' Moses told them. 'Collect what you need but no more. It is the food that God has provided.'

The people hurried to pick it up. It tasted like biscuits made with honey, and they called it 'manna'. They all had as much as they wanted; God gave them manna to eat every day while they were in the desert.

### Laws at Mount Sinai

The Hebrews journeyed southwards through the desert for many months until they came to a mountain called Sinai. They set up camp at its foot and Moses climbed the mountain alone to pray.

There God spoke to him. 'I promise to lead you all and look after you. I have chosen you for my own people and you must obey my laws.'

Moses went back and told the people what God had said. 'You must prepare yourselves to worship God,' he added. The people followed him to the foot of the mountain. A cloud covered Sinai. Thunder rumbled. Lightning and fire flashed and smoke billowed low. A trumpet peal sounded and the people trembled. 'The Lord God is here,' they whispered.

God spoke to Moses again. He gave him laws for the people to keep, so that they would behave in a way that pleased him.

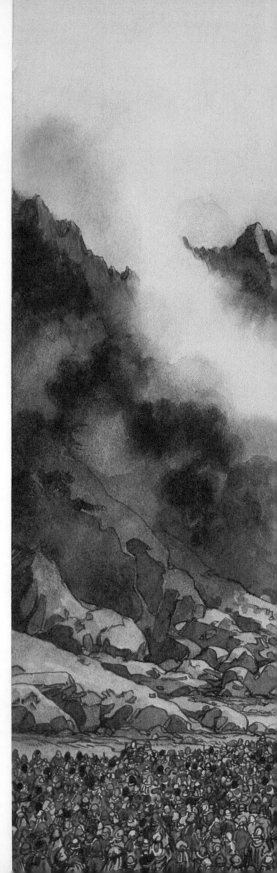

Moses told everyone what God had said. Then he went back up the mountain. This time he took one of his captains with him, a young man named Joshua.

### Aaron makes a gold bull

Moses and Joshua were away for a long time and the people grew frightened and impatient. 'The God Moses follows has taken him away. Let's choose a different god!' They begged Aaron, Moses' brother, to make them one. Aaron was frightened of the people, so he agreed. He collected their gold jewellery and melted it down. Then he foolishly made a statue of a bull from the molten gold.

Everyone was delighted. 'This is the god who brought us out of Egypt,' they cried. Although it was only lifeless metal they made a great feast in its honour. They brought it gifts and cheered and blew their trumpets.

By now, Moses and Joshua were on their way back. Moses carried two heavy slabs of stone on which God himself had written the new laws. They were surprised to hear singing and shouting in the camp. At first Joshua thought a fight had broken out, but Moses saw the golden statue and he grew very angry.

'God chose you to be his people. You promised not to make statues and worship them instead of God!' he shouted.

He smashed the stone slabs with God's laws on them to the ground. Then he ground down the statue to powder and mixed it with the drinking water so that the people had to drink it as a punishment. But he also prayed for the people. 'Forgive them, Lord God,' he begged.

'I don't break my promises,' said God. 'Cut two new slabs of stone like the ones you broke and I will give the people their laws again.'

Moses kept the new stone slabs in a special box covered with gold, and God told the people to make a beautiful tent to protect it when they set up camp. God himself would surround the tent in a special way, so it was to be called the Tent of God's Presence.

To make the tent the people all shared what they had. Some brought wood for the tentpoles. Others gave their jewellery. Weavers brought fine linen, woven with coloured threads, while others brought coarser cloth made of goat's hair. Some brought fine leather and rams' hides dyed

scarlet, while others brought spices, and oil for the lamp inside the tent. Then skilled craftsmen set to work to sew the cloth together, to make rings and fastenings and put up the tent. When it was ready a cloud covered it and a dazzling light shone through it. The people saw that God was with them. They fell on their faces and worshipped him.

At last they left Mount Sinai and went on with their long journey. The way was hard and they began to miss the green fields round the River Nile in Egypt. Very soon they were grumbling again. 'Do you remember the fish we ate in Egypt? We used to have cucumbers and watermelons, onions, leeks and garlic, too. Now we've nothing but manna for every meal!'

Moses overheard and he was angry. 'These people are impossible!' he told God. 'Where am I supposed to find meat for them all? I can't cope with their whining any more!'

'Moses, you need some helpers,' God said. 'I will choose leaders to help you, and I'll give everyone enough meat for a month!'

God did exactly as he promised. He chose seventy leaders to help Moses look after the tribes. Then a wind sprang up and carried a flock of little birds like partridges into the camp. They were quails, and, tired after their flight, they fell to the ground all round the people. All the Hebrews had to do was pick them up. That night everyone had meat for supper.

## The spies' story

Then they set off again, travelling towards the country of Canaan, the land God had promised them. By now they were very near. Moses sent out spies to grapes so heavy that it needed two men to carry it.

'Look!' they said, 'We picked these grapes, and pomegranates and figs, too. The land is very good, but the people are fierce and live in big cities with strong walls.

find out what sort of people lived there — fierce fighting men or wandering tribes.

The spies returned with news. They brought a great cluster of

We even saw giants who made us feel like grasshoppers!'

'Let's choose another leader and go back to Egypt!' everyone exclaimed in terror.

But Joshua, Moses' helper who had gone with the spies, cried, 'Don't be silly! God is fighting for us. He will help us conquer the land, giants and all!'

Another spy, called Caleb, agreed with Joshua, but the people refused to listen.

Suddenly a bright light shone from the Tent of God's Presence and God spoke. 'The people still don't trust me! Not one of them shall cross into the Promised Land except for Caleb and Joshua. They must go on wandering through the desert until they die. Then I shall give their land to their children.' Sadly the Hebrews set off from the edge of the Promised Land back into the desert.

### Forty years in the desert

In spite of everything, it wasn't long before they were grumbling again. They came to a place where there was no water, and instead of asking God to help them, they complained to Moses. He took Aaron with him to the Tent of the Presence to pray. Then they called everyone together in front of a huge rock. Moses struck it twice with his stick. Water spouted out, sparkling in the sunlight. Full of wonder, the people crowded round and drank thankfully.

Moses did not tell them it was God who made the water pour out of the rock. He hadn't been true to God, and now he would not be able to enter the Promised Land, either.

On their long journey the Hebrews crossed land belonging to many different tribes. Moses would send messengers to the rulers of each place explaining that they wanted to travel peacefully across his land without taking any food or water. Often, though, the ruler would meet them with an army, and then the Hebrews had to fight their way through.

A fierce king called Og heard that they were coming and set out to attack them. Og was a huge giant of a man, but the Hebrews were experienced fighters by now. 'God is on our side,' Joshua encouraged them. They defeated King Og and his army and captured his towns.

God gave them victory over everyone who tried to stop them. Forty years went by, and the people who had refused to trust God died. At last it was time to go into the Promised Land. Moses led the people to the banks of the River Jordan. On the other side lay their new country.

By now Aaron was dead and Moses was a very old man. He longed to lead the people into the new land, but he knew that God had said 'no'. From the top of a mountain called Pisgah, the Promised Land could be seen in the distance. God told Moses to climb the mountain. 'You will be able to see what the land is like,' he said. So Moses climbed the mountain. Brown desert hills rose sharply around him, but beyond the River Jordan shimmered the green valleys and hills of Canaan. Moses' eyesight was still good. He could see it all clearly. It was a fine land.

He went back to the camp singing God's praises. There he reminded everyone of the laws that they had promised to obey. Finally he blessed them all.

'No other nation is as blessed as you, because God has chosen you and he will keep you safe,' he said.

Then Moses died. The people were sad. They never forgot him.

'No one is greater than Moses because the Lord spoke to him face to face as a man speaks to his friend,' they said.

## Joshua, the new leader

Joshua, Moses' helper, became the new leader. At once he began to make plans for capturing Canaan. The first step was to take the town of Jericho which barred their way into the Promised Land. Joshua sent two spies across the Jordan. They slipped secretly into Jericho where they met a woman called Rahab who invited them to stay in her house which was perched between the walls. Someone spotted them and told the king, who sent his soldiers to the house. Rahab saw them coming and hid the spies on her flat roof under bundles of flax. Soon the soldiers were pounding on her door. 'Bring out those spies!' they yelled.

'What spies?' asked Rahab. 'Some men came by earlier, but they left the city when the gates shut at sunset. If you hurry you might catch them.'

Rahab laughed as she heard the gates open to let the soldiers out. She helped the spies to escape from her window down the outer wall.

'I'm doing this because I believe that your God is the true God,' she said. 'We have heard how he has helped you to win battles and the whole town is terrified. Promise you won't kill me or any of my family when you capture Jericho.'

The spies promised and gave her a red cord to mark the house. Then they hurried back to Joshua.

'Everyone is terrified of us! God will help us to win a tremendous victory!' they declared.

## Crossing the Jordan

First the people had to cross the River Jordan. They stared at the water, wondering how they would get across. Joshua called them together.

'God will help us,' he said. 'When you see the priests going down to the river carrying the gold box with the laws in it, follow them with all your belongings.'

The people did as Joshua said. When the priests stepped into the water the river stopped flowing, the water piled up to the north and dry land appeared.

Everyone crossed over safely. They chose twelve large stones from the river bed and set them up on the bank to remind everyone how they had crossed the river. Then they camped. For the first time there was no manna for them to eat. From now on they could eat the food of Canaan.

When the king of Jericho saw that the Hebrews were camping so close to the city he barred and bolted all the gates. Sentries guarded them, and no one was allowed to go in or out. One day Joshua was walking alone beside the city wondering how to attack it, when he saw a man standing in front of him holding an unsheathed sword.

'Are you one of our soldiers or an enemy?' Joshua challenged him.

'I am the commander of the army of the Lord God,' the stranger answered.

Then Joshua remembered what Moses had said to him before he died. 'Be strong, Joshua, and full of courage, for God himself goes with you and he will never ever fail you.'

Joshua bowed his face to the ground and said to the man, 'I am your servant. Give me your orders, Commander.'

'Take off your sandals, this is holy ground.' Joshua obeyed. Now he knew for sure that they would capture the town. Later God spoke to Joshua and told him exactly what to do.

### Victory in Jericho

The Hebrews didn't storm the walls or batter down the gates. Instead they marched round the city; first a guard of soldiers, then seven priests blowing their trumpets, then more priests carrying the precious box, and the army tramping behind in silence. They did the same thing for seven days, while the people of Jericho laughed and jeered at them from their high walls.

On the seventh day they marched seven times right round the walls. Then Joshua yelled, 'God has given us the city!' and the people cheered and blew their trumpets.

At once the houses and towers along the wall began to topple. With a loud rumble the walls smashed down, and the Hebrews poured into Jericho, yelling and cheering. They found Rahab and her family and led them safely out of their ruined home, but they destroyed the rest of the city.

The news spread like wildfire. Soon Joshua and the Hebrews were feared all over Canaan. They began to capture the rest of the land and settle in the country that God had given them.

# GIDEON

## A mighty hero

After the Hebrews had driven their enemies out of Canaan and settled the land, they still did not enjoy peace. To make matters worse, as time went by and Joshua and the men and the women who had known him grew old and died, their children and grandchildren began to forget God and worship other gods. When enemies attacked them they did not ask God for help and God often let their enemies defeat them.

The Midianites were among their fiercest enemies. They were wild tribesmen who had learned how to ride on camels when they went to war. They made surprise attacks on the Israelites, as the people were known now.

The Israelites had to leave their farms and hide whenever the Midianites came to raid them.

At last, when this had been going on for seven years, the people remembered God and turned to him for help. God heard them and sent an angel to a man called Gideon.

Gideon was threshing wheat, secretly, because he was afraid of the Midianites, when the angel spoke to him. 'God is with you, mighty hero! Go and defeat the Midianites!'

'How can I do that?' Gideon wondered.

'Easily, because God will help you,' the angel answered.

But Gideon was afraid. 'But how do I know that?' he exclaimed. 'My family is poor. I'm not an important person. I shall need proof.'

He brought bread and meat and put them on a rock before the stranger. The angel touched them with the end of his long stick. Fire spurted out of the rock and burnt up the food. The angel vanished and Gideon was left, shaking with fright.

'Don't be afraid,' God said. Gideon felt braver. He knelt and worshipped God.

Although the Israelites had asked God for help, many of them, including Gideon's father, still worshipped statues of gold or wood which they said were gods. That night God spoke to Gideon again. 'Pull down the statue your father worships and chop it up for firewood. Then break down his altar, build one for me, and bring a bull as an offering.'

So that night Gideon and his servants secretly harnessed one of his father's bullocks. They tied ropes to the idol's altar and they tore it down with a loud thud.

They worked in the dark because Gideon was afraid of his family.

In the morning there was a great outcry when the people discovered that their god had been chopped down. They questioned everyone until they found out who had done it. 'Kill Gideon! He's destroyed our god!' they yelled, but Gideon's father said, 'Let the god speak up for himself. After all, it was his altar that was pulled down!'

So Gideon was kept safe, for of course the statue could not harm him.

## Gideon and the sheepskin

But Gideon still wasn't sure. Had God really chosen him to fight the powerful Midianites?

One evening he took a sheepskin and laid it on the ground. 'If the ground is bone dry in the morning but the wool is drenched with dew I'll know that God will help me,' Gideon said.

He got up early next morning, just as the birds were starting to sing, and picked up the fleece. It was sodden and heavy. When he wrung it out a bowlful of water splashed to the ground, but the grass around the fleece was quite dry.

'Do it once more, Lord,' Gideon prayed. 'This time let the wool stay dry and the ground wet. Then I'll know you really will use me against the Midianites.'

Next morning Gideon's feet were soaked as he crossed the wet ground, but the wool was still curly and dry. At last Gideon was convinced that God would help him, and he got ready for battle.

## Gideon's small army

Gideon gathered as many men as he could find but God said, 'There are too many men in this army. Tell everyone who's feeling scared to go home.' Twenty thousand men went home and ten thousand were left. 'There are still too many.' God said. 'Here's a test for them. Tell them all to go to the stream and have a drink.' Gideon watched the men drink. Some knelt down and put their faces in the water, lapping like dogs, but three hundred men scooped the water up in their cupped hands and drank looking round them. God told Gideon to choose them.

So Gideon took his three hundred men to fight the Midianites who were camped below them in a valley. Their tents dotted the ground like a thick swarm of buzzing insects.

Gideon still found it hard to believe that God would really use him to defeat such a large army.

God told Gideon to go secretly to the Midianite camp. There Gideon heard a man tell his friend, 'I dreamed that God gave Gideon victory over our whole army.'

Gideon knelt down in the darkness and thanked God. He was convinced now! He rushed back to his men. 'Get up! Get up! God will win the battle for us,' he said. They crept down to the valley. Each man carried a trumpet and a heavy earthenware pot with a flaming branch hidden inside it.

They took up their positions around the camp. Just before midnight Gideon yelled his war cry, 'For the Lord and for Gideon!' He smashed the jar and blew his trumpet. His men did the same. Torches flared in the darkness. The sudden din threw the sleepy Midianites into confusion. Baffled by the flares and the blast of trumpets and the crashing pots they were sure a huge army had attacked them. They pulled out their swords, but in the darkness they started to attack their own men. The Midianites ran away into the night, fighting one another while Gideon's men waited, blowing their trumpets until the powerful Midianite army destroyed itself in panic. Then Gideon's army, joined by other Israelite tribes, chased the fleeing enemies away from Canaan. The Israelites were overjoyed and wanted to make Gideon their king.

Gideon refused. 'I won't rule over you and neither shall my son. The Lord God who won this victory is the ruler we must obey,'

he said. 'You can give me a present, though. Let me have the gold ear-rings you've plundered.'

The Midianites all wore gold ear-rings and the Israelites had stripped them from their defeated enemy. They were only too pleased to give their booty to Gideon. A large cloth was spread out and was soon full of ear-rings as well as the necklets and armbands worn by the kings of Midian and the gold collars from their camels, all clinking together. Gideon melted the gold down and made it into a statue which he set up in his home town. Although Gideon's great victory brought peace to Israel many people turned away from God and worshipped the golden statue. In the end it brought harm to Gideon's family, but Gideon himself lived happily till the end of his days and never had to hide from the Midianites again.

# SAMSON

## Invaders from the sea

Many years later other strong invaders came and conquered Canaan. These were the Philistines, a sea people who came in their ships with swords and spears of iron. The weapons the Israelites had weren't nearly as strong.

God's people needed help again, so one day God sent an angel to a married couple who had no children.

'You will have a son who is to be kept specially for God,' the angel told them. 'He must never drink beer or wine. He must never touch anything dead, and he must never cut his hair.'

When the boy was born his parents called him Samson. God blessed him and made him very strong so that he could fight the Philistines single handed and protect his country. But in the end Samson did not use his strength wisely. He fell in love with a Philistine girl and refused to listen when his parents begged him not to marry her. 'I like her. Get her for me,' he said, and went off to meet her. On his way Samson heard the roar of a young lion. He swung round. There stood the lion, snarling at him, ready to pounce.

Samson had no weapons, but he killed the lion with his bare hands as easily as if it had been a young goat. Then he went on to meet the girl and arrange the wedding. He didn't tell anyone about the lion.

Samson went home to fetch his parents to the wedding. As they

passed the place where he had killed the lion, a swarm of bees buzzed round the skeleton. Samson scooped a honeycomb out of the bones and enjoyed the fresh honey. He gave some to his parents but they didn't see where he found it and he didn't tell them.

### Samson's riddle

So they went on to meet the bride and Samson gave a party. Thirty young Philistine men joined the feast. Samson made up a riddle for them. 'Out of the eater came what is eaten and out of the strong came what is sweet,' he said. 'Guess my riddle and I'll give you each two suits of fine linen. But if you can't guess by the end of the week when the feast is over each of you must give me two suits of linen.' They agreed but they couldn't puzzle out the meaning at all. At last they went to Samson's bride. 'Tell us the meaning or we'll burn the house down with you inside it,' they threatened.

So the girl begged Samson to tell her the answer. In the end he told her, and at once she informed the Philistines. On the last day of the feast they came to Samson.

'We've guessed your riddle. It was easy!' they said. 'What can be sweeter than honey and what can be stronger than the lion you took the honey from?'

Samson was so furious that he marched off to one of the Philistine towns, killed thirty men and stole their clothes. He gave them to the wedding guests and stormed home. His bride was quickly married off to the best man. When Samson heard this he set fire to the Philistines' cornfields and olive trees and ruined their harvest.

A thousand Philistines attacked the Israelites. 'Give us Samson and we'll leave you alone,' they said. The Israelites found Samson. 'You've stirred the Philistines up against us. They're far stronger than we are. We're in real trouble and we've come to hand you over to them.'

'That's all right so long as you promise not to kill me first,' agreed Samson. He allowed them to tie him up with two strong new ropes and take him out to the

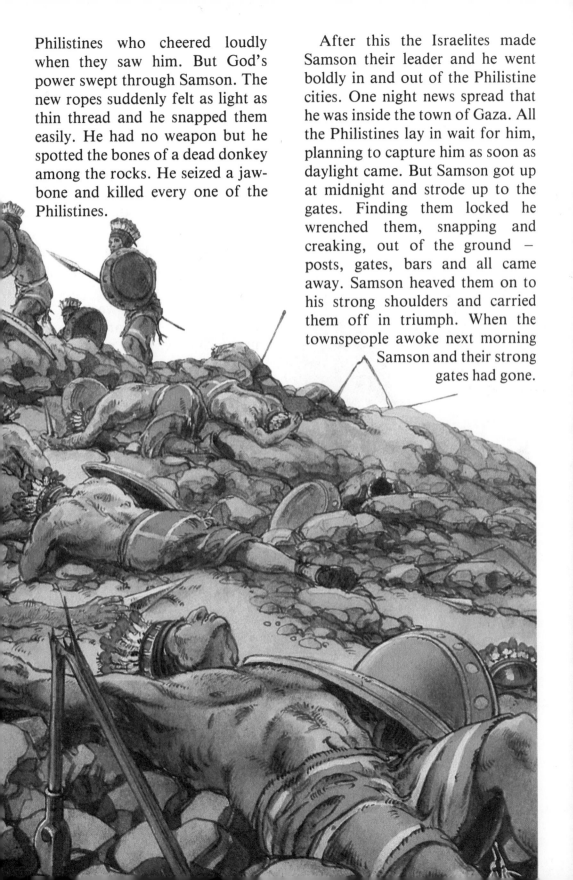

Philistines who cheered loudly when they saw him. But God's power swept through Samson. The new ropes suddenly felt as light as thin thread and he snapped them easily. He had no weapon but he spotted the bones of a dead donkey among the rocks. He seized a jawbone and killed every one of the Philistines.

After this the Israelites made Samson their leader and he went boldly in and out of the Philistine cities. One night news spread that he was inside the town of Gaza. All the Philistines lay in wait for him, planning to capture him as soon as daylight came. But Samson got up at midnight and strode up to the gates. Finding them locked he wrenched them, snapping and creaking, out of the ground – posts, gates, bars and all came away. Samson heaved them on to his strong shoulders and carried them off in triumph. When the townspeople awoke next morning Samson and their strong gates had gone.

But although Samson was so strong, he had weaknesses. One of them was that he couldn't keep a secret. He fell in love with another Philistine girl whose name was Delilah, and the Philistine chiefs promised to pay her eleven hundred silver pieces if she told them the secret of Samson's strength. At first he tricked her. 'Tie me with seven new bowstrings and I'll be helpless,' he said. The Philistine chiefs brought Delilah the bowstrings and hid outside the room. She tied Samson as he slept. 'Quick, wake up, Samson, the Philistines are upon you!' she yelled.

The chiefs crowded into the room. Samson leapt to his feet. He laughed and snapped the bowstrings easily.

Delilah burst into tears. 'You've made a fool of me with your lies, tell me the truth this time.' He tricked her twice more, and she cried and told him that he didn't really love her. In the end he told her his secret.

'From the moment I was born I was kept apart for God. My hair has never been cut. Shave my hair and I'll be as weak as anyone else. Now are you happy? You've worn me out with all your pleading and crying!'

Delilah soothed him to sleep. She beckoned a man who cut seven long locks of hair from Samson's head. Then she called loudly, 'Wake up, Samson. The Philistines are upon you!' The chiefs burst into the room. Samson awoke perplexed, and they captured him easily, for without his hair all his strength had gone.

Now the Philistines treated Samson cruelly. They put out his eyes, bound him with heavy bronze chains and made him their slave as well as their prisoner. He had to kneel on the ground all day, grinding grain with a round stone roller. But the Philistines didn't notice that Samson's hair had begun to grow again.

To celebrate their capture the Philistine chiefs gathered in the temple of Dagon, the god they worshipped. Thousands of people crowded into the temple and climbed up on the roof to watch the ceremonies. 'Let's get Samson out and have some fun!' they shouted.

They laughed and jeered as they watched blind Samson stumble along, led by a little boy. They made him stand right in the middle of the temple between the pillars that held up the entire roof. Samson said softly to the boy, 'Let me feel where the pillars are and lean against them for a moment.'

He stretched out his hands and touched the pillars. He looked up. He could see nothing now, but he knew God was there in the darkness. 'Give me my strength this once, Lord,' he prayed. He stretched his arms out to the pillars and braced his shoulders. The pillars tottered as Samson pushed them; great blocks of stone rumbled and crashed together and the great roof fell in, burying Samson and his enemies in the ruins of the temple.

When the Israelites heard, they praised Samson. 'He killed more Philistines in his death than in his life,' they said. But they still needed a leader who would drive their enemies away for good.

# RUTH

### Famine in Israel

Although the Israelites were often in danger from their enemies during these years after they had entered Canaan, they were not always fighting. Then they had other problems to face! One year the harvest was so bad that there wasn't enough food for everyone. One of the Israelites decided to move with his wife, Naomi, and two sons to another country where the harvest was good. There was plenty of corn in Moab, so the family settled there. Time went by and the two boys grew up and married two Moabite girls called Ruth and Orpah. They were all very happy, but before long a great sadness came to the little family. First Naomi's husband died and then, soon afterwards her two sons died as well. Poor Naomi was left alone, far from home.

She called her daughters-in-law to her. 'You must think of yourselves now,' she told them. 'Go home to your families. I'm sure they'll be able to find new husbands for you. Don't worry about me. I'll go back home to Israel.'

'But we want to go with you,' the girls said. So they packed their belongings and set off. Before they reached the borders of Israel, Naomi tried once more to persuade the girls to leave her and go back home.

At last Orpah agreed and turned for home, but Ruth refused to leave. 'I want to stay with you,' she said. 'I will make my home in your country, and worship your God. Don't keep asking me to go away.' When Naomi saw that Ruth really meant what she said, she was pleased, for she had no other friend, and so they went on together, journeying towards Israel.

At last they arrived at Bethlehem, the town where Naomi used to live. It was harvest time, and the town's white walls rose up in front of them from fields of rustling barley. The families who were gathering the harvest straightened up and shaded their eyes as the two women went by. 'Isn't that Naomi, come home after all these years?' they cried. 'How sad she looks! Where are her husband and sons? There's only a foreign girl with her.'

They crowded on to the road to meet her and hear her story.

## Ruth and Boaz

Ruth and Naomi were very poor, but they managed to find somewhere to live in Bethlehem. Then they had to think about food. They had no money to buy grain, but God had given the Israelites a law, which said that poor people should be allowed to walk behind the men who reaped in the harvest and pick up all the grain they left behind.

When Ruth heard about this she asked Naomi if she might go and gather grain for them. Naomi agreed, and Ruth set out early in the morning to follow the harvesters.

The field where she was working belonged to a rich farmer called Boaz. He was very impressed when he heard Ruth's story.

'She's a kind girl to leave her own home and look after Naomi.

Make sure she gets enough grain,' he told his men. 'Pull some from your own bundles and put it in her path.'

That evening Ruth brought home a huge bundle of barley. She ground it into flour and Naomi baked hot tasty bread. When Naomi heard where Ruth had been working she was delighted. 'Boaz is related to us,' she exclaimed. 'In fact he must be my nearest relation

now. Perhaps he'll do something to help us. You must go back to his field tomorrow.'

So every day through the harvest, Ruth went to the same field, and every day Boaz watched for her. He saw how hard she worked and how gentle she was with everybody. By the end of the harvest he was in love with her, and before the last of the grain was threshed they were married.

By the time the barley was ripe next year Ruth had a baby boy. They called him Obed. Now Naomi was happy. She loved Ruth's baby as though he were her own son. She would have been even happier if she had known that when Obed was grown up his grandson would become Israel's greatest king, King David, and that Ruth the foreign girl would have become part of Israel's history.

# SAMUEL

### Hannah's promise

About the time that Ruth's baby, Obed, was born there lived in another part of the country, a woman called Hannah.

Every year she went to the Temple at Shiloh with her husband to worship God. One year, when everyone else was feasting. Hannah slipped away by herself to the Temple to pray. She was unhappy because she had no children and the other women laughed at her. She cried as she prayed, 'Please God, give me a son. I promise I'll give him back to you so that he can serve you all his life.' Hannah's voice could not be heard – only her lips were moving. Eli the priest was watching her and thought she was drunk. 'Enough of this drunken behaviour,' he said sternly. 'This is no place for you. Come back when you are sober.'

'Oh sir,' answered Hannah, 'I'm not drunk. I'm pouring out my troubles to God.'

'Then go in peace,' said Eli, 'and may God give you whatever you asked for.'

Before the year was over, Hannah had a baby boy. She called him Samuel. She was very happy, and she didn't forget her promise to God. When he was still quite small, no more than four or five years old, she took him to the Temple to see Eli.

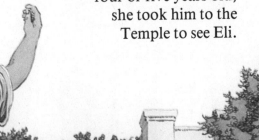

The old man looked down at the boy. 'Who is this?' he asked. 'This is the son I prayed for,' said Hannah. 'Now I have come to give him to the Lord so that he can serve God always.'

So it was arranged. Samuel was to stay in the Temple as Eli's helper, but his mother was to visit him and make him new clothes as he grew out of his old ones.

So every year Hannah came to visit Samuel. She brought him new clothes, and told him all the news from home and later she brought his younger brothers and sisters to see him, for Hannah had five more children after Samuel. Samuel enjoyed showing them the Temple and telling them how he tried to please God. Hannah was very happy. She could see that Samuel felt quite at home in the Temple.

## A voice in the night

Eli's sons were priests in the Temple, but they were cheats who stole the offerings which poor people brought for God. Eli knew what was going on, but he would not stop his sons. Then, late one night, as Samuel was lying on his sleeping mat near the big seven-branched candlestick in the Temple, he heard a voice calling him, 'Samuel, Samuel!'

The boy sat up. The lamps were still burning. He peered beyond the steady flames, but he couldn't see anyone. He decided Eli must have called and he ran over to him, but Eli said, 'Go back to sleep, Samuel, I didn't call you.'

Samuel lay down, but the voice called his name again. He ran back to Eli.

'You did call me, sir,' he insisted.

'No I didn't,' the old man replied. 'Go back to sleep.'

So Samuel went back to bed, but the voice called again and he went and told Eli.

Now the old priest realised that God was trying to speak to Samuel.

'If the voice calls again, say, "Speak Lord, your servant is listening," ' Eli said.

So Samuel lay down again and when the voice spoke once more he answered clearly, 'Speak Lord, your servant is listening.'

'You must tell Eli that I shall punish his sons because they have turned against me,' said God.

The next morning, when Eli asked Samuel 'What did the Lord say to you?' Samuel didn't want to tell Eli what God had said, but at last he was persuaded to speak. When Eli heard God's message, he said simply, 'He is God, he must do as he thinks right.'

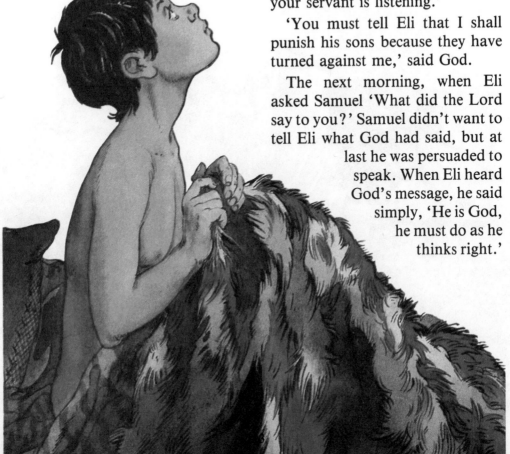

### Capture of the covenant box

Soon afterwards the Philistines attacked the Israelites and defeated them in a terrible battle. Some of the Israelites fled to the Temple at Shiloh. They wanted to take the holy covenant box, which held the stone slabs inscribed with God's promises, away to the battlefield. They thought it would help them win because it was a sign that God was with them. Eli's sons carried the box to the army camp.

When the soldiers on the battlefield saw the box they cheered so loudly that the Philistines attacked even harder. They killed thirty thousand men, including Eli's sons, and captured the precious box. God would not help Israel to win because the people had turned away from him.

A messenger came running to bring Eli the news. The old priest was sitting by the gates of the town waiting anxiously to hear how the battle had gone. When he heard that his sons were dead and the sacred box had been captured he fell backwards from his chair and died.

However, God did not let the Philistines keep the covenant box for long. Disease and plagues spread through every city where they tried to keep it. Before long the Philistines had had enough. They put the box onto a wooden cart and loaded gifts of gold round it. Then they hitched two cows to the cart and sent them off. The cows headed straight towards Israel.

The Israelites were overjoyed to have their covenant box back, but the Philistines still kept attacking them. At last they remembered God, and prayed for his help.

Samuel, who was now one of the most respected men in Israel, gathered everyone together.

'God will only rescue you if you get rid of all these idols you worship and turn back to him,' Samuel told them.

The people really were sorry that they had turned away from God.

They poured water over the ground and ate no food as a sign that they knew they had done wrong, and Samuel prayed for them. Then God helped the Israelites to win back all the cities the Philistines had captured.

# SAUL

## *The people ask for a king*

In spite of the successes that God gave to the Israelites in battle, the people began to grumble.

'Other countries have kings who lead them out to battle,' they complained to the prophet Samuel. 'Give us a king, too!' Samuel was very upset, and prayed to God.

'Don't be upset,' God replied.

'It isn't *you* the people are rejecting. It's me. Do as they say and let them have a king, but warn them that it won't be easy for them.'

Samuel told the people what God had said.

'Do you know how your king will treat you?' he asked. 'He'll take your sons and daughters and make them work for him. He'll take your best fields and your strongest cattle and donkeys, too.'

But the people wanted a king so much that they wouldn't listen to Samuel, so he waited for God to show him whom he should choose to be king.

Soon afterwards a young stranger entered the city where Samuel was living. 'He's your man,' said the Lord to Samuel, 'he is the new king.' Samuel welcomed the stranger warmly.

The young man, whose name was Saul, was astonished. He had been looking for Samuel to ask his help to find some of his father's donkeys which were lost. He didn't expect such a kind welcome, and he was even more amazed when Samuel seemed to know about his errand without being told. 'Don't worry about the donkeys, they've been found,' Samuel told him, and he invited the young man and his servant to eat with him and spend the night at his house.

Early next morning, before anyone was up to see what was happening, Samuel anointed Saul king of Israel, taking a horn full of oil and pouring it over his head.

'This oil,' he said, 'is a sign that God has chosen you.'

Later Samuel planned to present Saul to the people, but when all the Israelites were gathered together the young man was nowhere to be found. He was hiding among the baggage and stores. They had to search for him and lead him out.

Saul looked like a king for he was a head taller than anyone else. As soon as they saw him everyone shouted 'Long live King Saul! God save the King!' But some people still wondered if Saul would be able to help them. 'He doesn't come from a rich important family,' they grumbled and they refused to follow him.

To start with, however, Saul did well. Just after he became king, a fierce tribe called the Ammonites attacked the town of Jabesh. The Ammonite leader warned the townsfolk that even if they surrendered at once he would still put out everyone's right eye. At once the men of Jabesh sent an urgent message to Saul.

Saul was angry. He wanted to rush off and help the people of Jabesh immediately but first he had to make sure that all the Israelites would follow him.

He killed two oxen and chopped them in pieces. Then he sent messengers up and down the country carrying the pieces.

'Saul will chop up your oxen like this if you refuse to follow him,' the messengers warned.

A large army gathered at once and Saul led them to Jabesh. The battle began at dawn the next day. By midday Saul and his men had won a great victory. The Israelites were delighted and wanted to kill the men who had not wanted Saul to be king. But Saul said, 'There's to be no killing today, now that God has given us victory.'

'Let's go to Gilgal,' added Samuel, 'we'll give Saul a proper coronation.' So they all went up to the holy place at Gilgal and held a great celebration in Saul's honour.

### Saul disobeys God

Samuel hoped that Saul would go on being a good king, but he was disappointed. One day Saul's son, Jonathan, attacked a Philistine outpost and the Philistines launched a full scale attack in revenge. Saul gathered a large army to fight them, but Samuel told them to wait for him to come and offer sacrifices to God before they went into battle. They waited for a whole week and Samuel didn't come. The people were frightened because the Philistines were getting closer and the army wasn't ready to fight.

Some of the men began to slink off home and Saul grew impatient. At last he made the sacrifice himself. Just as he was finishing Samuel arrived. He was furious. 'Why couldn't you wait as I asked?' he demanded. 'You've disobeyed God and acted foolishly by offering the sacrifice yourself. Now he will find someone else to be king instead of you – someone who will obey him.'

A little later Samuel gave Saul another command from God: 'Attack the tribe called the Amalekites and destroy them all. Don't leave anything alive, either people or animals.'

Saul went to battle and defeated the Amalekites, but he kept the king as a prisoner and saved the best cattle and sheep as booty for his soldiers.

Samuel came to the camp to visit Saul.

'You've disobeyed God again,' he cried angrily, 'I can hear cows mooing and sheep bleating.'

'I did what God said,' lied Saul. 'I just kept the best animals to sacrifice to the Lord.'

'It's better to obey God than to offer even the best sheep to him,' Samuel replied. 'Because you have rejected God by disobeying him, he will reject you.'

As Samuel turned away, Saul clutched the old man's cloak, begging him to stay. There was a sound of ripping cloth, and the cloak tore in his grasp.

'God has torn your kingdom from you and given it to someone else,' said Samuel.

Saul faced him in despair. 'I've done wrong, but I'm still the leader of Israel. Don't show me up in front of my army,' he begged.

Samuel relented. They worshipped God together and then Samuel left. He felt sorry for Saul, who was left to rule alone without God's help. They never saw each other again.

# DAVID THE SHEPHERD KING

### *God chooses a new king*

Because King Saul had disobeyed God so many times, God told Samuel to choose a new king. It was a dangerous thing to do, for if Saul heard about it, Samuel knew he would kill him. The old man had to be very careful.

'Go to Bethlehem,' God told him. 'A man called Jesse lives there and I have chosen one of his sons to be king. Take a calf and sacrifice it to me there so that Saul won't be suspicious, and I will tell you what else to do.'

So Samuel went to Bethlehem and invited Jesse and his sons to the sacrifice. Jesse's eldest son was strong and handsome – Samuel would have chosen him for king at once, but God said, 'No'. It was the same with his six younger brothers – God didn't want any of them to be king.

'Haven't you any more children?' Samuel asked.

'There's my youngest, David, but he's looking after the sheep,' replied Jesse.

He sent a servant to fetch David.

'I like the look of him,' Samuel thought, watching David's eager, flushed face. 'Could this be the one?'

'Yes,' came God's answer. 'Pour oil on his head now as a sign that I have chosen him to be king.'

Samuel poured oil on David's bent head. David looked up. His eyes shone. 'This young man loves God,' Samuel thought. 'God will help him to be the right kind of king.'

Meanwhile, Saul was filled with despair for he knew that God had left him. He began to have black moods when no one could comfort

him. His servants saw how sad he was and said to him, 'Why don't you look for someone to play music to you? That will calm you, and make you feel happier.'

Saul agreed, and one of his servants spoke up, 'I've heard of a young shepherd called David who can play the harp and sing well. Why don't you send for him?'

So David arrived at the palace as Saul's servant. He brought presents for the king: a donkey loaded with fresh bread and wine, and a white, bleating kid. But the best present for Saul was David's music. He sang about the high hills round his home where he wandered with his sheep. Best of all he sang about God. Whenever a black mood came upon Saul, David would play for him, and Saul would feel better.

Before long, David had to go

back to Bethlehem to look after his father's sheep. He was a good shepherd — he took great care of his flock and protected it from danger. Wild animals often tried to carry off the sheep to eat. David would hear the bleating of a frightened lamb and look up to see a mountain bear or a lion standing over it, ready to eat it. Without a second thought David would rush after the animal and attack it, battering it with his club or fighting it with his bare hands, snatching the lamb from the animal's mouth.

### David kills Goliath

Soon after David's visit to the palace, Israel's enemies, the Philistines, attacked Saul and his army. David's brothers had to go to fight, but David stayed at home to look after the sheep.

From time to time Jesse would send him to Saul's camp to find out how his brothers were and take them some extra food.

One day when David arrived he found the whole army lined up watching one of the Philistines, a massive giant, three metres tall, wearing a helmet and heavy armour. His name was Goliath of Gath. He was strutting up and down the valley between the two armies, jeering at Saul's men, as he had done nearly every day since the armies camped there.

'Choose a man to fight me. We'll decide the battle with a single blow!' he yelled. But none of the Israelites dared to fight the Philistine.

'Who does that man think he is?' demanded David.

'He's not only insulting our army, he's insulting God, too.'

'What do you know about it?' growled David's eldest brother. 'Get back to your sheep, you cheeky brat!'

'Can't I even ask a simple question?' returned David. 'Is the king offering a reward to the man who kills that giant?' he went on.

'Yes, he is,' put in one of the soldiers. 'Are you interested?'

Everyone laughed. Someone overheard what was going on and told Saul. The king sent for David.

'Why, it's the shepherd!' the king exclaimed. 'What do you want, David?'

'Your Majesty, I'm not scared of that Philistine. I'll go and fight him.'

'You, David? No, you can't possibly do that,' replied Saul. 'You're too young. He's bigger than you, and besides he's a trained soldier.'

'Sir, I have to take my father's sheep high in the hills. Often the lions and bears try to snatch the lambs from the flock. I've killed them, sir, and I'll kill this Philistine, too. God helped me then and he'll keep me safe now!'

'All right, David,' Saul said. 'Go and fight the giant, and may God help you! You'd better take my armour.'

The king put his helmet on David's head and gave him his armour and sword, but David hesitated.

'I'm sorry, sir,' he said, 'But I've never fought in armour before.' Then he picked up his shepherd's stick and his sling instead, and choosing five smooth pebbles from the brook that ran through the camp, he walked down into the valley to meet Goliath.

The Philistine laughed. 'Hey, they've sent a young lad to fight me! What do you think I am?

A dog to be chased off with your sticks and stones?'

He began to curse David in the name of his god, but David yelled back, 'You've got a spear, a sword and a javelin to fight me with, but I'm going to fight you with the help of God, and he's stronger than you or your army!'

Furious, Goliath strode towards David, who quickly slipped a stone into his sling and hurled it at the Philistine. It hit his forehead and the giant reeled and fell heavily on his face. David jumped on the body, tugged Goliath's heavy iron sword out of its scabbard and cut off his head. When the Philistines saw what had happened they fled in confusion, and the cheering Israelites chased them all the way back to their own country. It was a complete victory! Saul made David one of his captains that very day and no one was more delighted than Saul's son, Prince Jonathan, who was a brave soldier.

'I'll never forget today as long as I live!' said Jonathan. 'Now your father will have to look for another shepherd, though it won't be easy to find anyone as brave as you!' Jonathan took off his royal robe and put it on David. Then he gave the shepherd his own armour and weapons: his sword and bow and arrows and belt.

'Take them, David, they're yours now,' declared Jonathan. He promised to be friends with David for ever.

131

### Saul the jealous king

After the battle the women came out of their villages to meet Saul, dancing round him, shaking their tambourines and singing to celebrate the victory, but the words they sang made Saul jealous.

'Saul has killed thousands of men, but David has killed tens of thousands!'

'They'll make David king instead of me!' muttered Saul. He rode home in a very bad temper and from then on he was too jealous of David ever to trust him again.

The next day Saul was in one of his black moods and David sat beside him playing his harp. Suddenly Saul grabbed a javelin and hurled it at David, meaning to pin him to the wall. David dodged and the javelin missed him, but Saul still wanted to kill David. He sent him to fight against the Philistines, hoping he would be killed in battle, but David led the army so well that he won great victories and became more popular than ever.

Saul was now so jealous that he tried to get Jonathan's help to kill David. Jonathan was always loyal to his father, but he spoke up bravely for his friend. Saul listened to him and promised not to hurt David any more, but before long he was plotting against him again.

David knew his life was in danger, although Jonathan could not believe that his father had gone back on his word.

Together they decided to find out if Saul really was planning David's death, for David knew that Jonathan was the only person he could trust.

'You hide behind the rock,' Jonathan told David. 'I'll find out how my father feels about you, and I'll come back here. I'll bring my arrows and pretend that I'm shooting at a target for practice. If you hear me tell my servant that the arrows have fallen beyond the target you'll know that my father really is planning to kill you.'

When Jonathan tried to talk to the king about David, Saul turned on him furiously.

'That shepherd's trying to steal my throne and he's taken you in completely, you fool. Don't you realise that you'll never be king after me as long as David's alive?' In his rage Saul tried to kill Jonathan, too, but the prince slipped away with a servant boy

and went to find David. Out in the field he started shooting his arrows near the rock.

'Look, the arrow's fallen further on. Run and find it,' Jonathan called to his servant.

As soon as the boy was out of sight David ran to Jonathan. He

knelt down and bowed to the ground three times before the prince. They were both in tears as they said goodbye to each other.

'We'll always be friends and so will our children,' Jonathan promised. 'God go with you, David.'

Then David went into hiding and Jonathan returned slowly home.

### David spares Saul's life

Saul was furious when he heard how David had escaped. He set out with his army and chased him, but before he could find him, a small band of outlaws and men who did not want to serve Saul joined David. They lived in secret caves in the hills. One day a man appeared in the opening of the very cave where David was hiding.

'It's the king,' whispered David's men. 'Come on, David. This is your chance. Kill him now.'

David crept forward in the darkness, sword in hand. He stopped behind Saul, bent forward and slashed a corner off the king's long cloak while his men stared, dumbfounded.

'I'll never harm Saul,' David explained when he rejoined his men. 'God chose him to rule over us.'

So Saul walked out of the cave safely, with no idea of the danger he had been in until he heard a voice call out 'Your Majesty!'

Saul spun round in amazement. David dropped to his knees.

'Sir, why do you keep on trying to kill me? I could have killed you just now, but I only cut a corner off your cloak. Look, here it is! Doesn't that convince you? You are my king, sir, and I'll never harm a hair of your head.'

'Oh, David, can that really be you?' Saul exclaimed. Suddenly he burst into tears. 'I realise how wrong I've been about you. You're a better man than I am. You have protected me and I have tried to hurt you. I won't any more.'

But Saul soon forgot his promise and sent his army out after David again.

Saul was very lonely now. His black moods of despair stayed with him nearly all the time, for there was no David to drive them away with music. The Philistines, whom David had helped to defeat, attacked him once more with a huge army. In his trouble and terror Saul did one last desperate thing. He knew that black magic was forbidden by God, but one night he disguised himself and went to visit a woman who claimed to be able to speak to the dead.

'I want to speak to the ghost of Samuel,' he told her. Samuel had been dead for many years, but Saul hoped his ghost might still help him with his problem.

When the shadowy figure of Samuel appeared, however, he gave Saul a terrible warning. 'You will lose the battle with the Philistines,' he said, 'and tomorrow you and your sons will be with me.'

So Saul went to his last fight, and there, at the battle of Mount Gilboa, Jonathan and Saul's other sons were killed.

Then Saul himself was wounded by an arrow. He knew he could not escape and he did not want to be captured by the jeering Philistines, so he fell on his own sword and killed himself.

When David heard the news he was overcome with grief in spite of everything that Saul had done to him. He tore his clothes as a sign of sorrow and he and his men ate no food until the evening. Then David picked up his harp and sang a lament for Saul and his dear dead friend Jonathan.

Daughters of Israel, sorrow for Saul who gave you brooches of gold and clothed you so well;

Now he is dead on the battlefield; let no dew or rain fall!
For Jonathan's dead and Saul's with him lying: they were swifter than eagles, far stronger than lions; dear to me, lovely, not divided in dying.
High on the mountains our heroes all fell.
Why did your weapons fail you, O Israel?

### King David captures Jerusalem

After Saul's death the people of Israel made David king. At first he ruled the people from the town of Hebron, but he had no proper capital city. Then one day he and his men went to attack a fortress which belonged to Israel's enemies, the Jebusites.

'You'll never capture us,' jeered the Jebusites. 'We've built our fort on solid rock. There are steep precipices on three sides of us, and the walls on the fourth side are too strong for you.'

They were right, but there was one way into the city, and David discovered it.

'They've dug a secret tunnel right under the walls to their water

supply outside the fort,' he told his men. 'We can go up it.'

Some of the soldiers crawled along the water channel that led up a steep shaft in the rock and along a tunnel right into the fortress. Then they opened the city gates and let in the rest of David's army.

So David captured the fortress and built his capital city there. Its name was Jerusalem, and there is a city on this spot to this day. From Jerusalem David ruled his kingdom and made it strong.

David didn't forget his friend Jonathan. One day he asked Saul's old servants if anyone in Jonathan's family was left alive.

'There is someone,' replied one

of the men. 'He's Jonathan's son, sir. He's lame.'

'Fetch him here to me,' David ordered, and the men went to look for him.

Some days later the servants announced to King David: 'Here is Mephibosheth, Jonathan's son!' Mephibosheth limped slowly into David's room. He greeted David politely and knelt in front of the king. David could tell that he was frightened. He spoke gently to his best friend's only son.

'Don't be afraid, Mephibosheth. I haven't brought you here to harm you, but to see if I can help you.

I'm going to give you back all the farms which your grandfather Saul owned. You shall have servants to look after them for you.' Mephibosheth looked up at David in amazement.

'I'm too lame to fight for you, sir, and my grandfather kept trying to kill you. I thought you would treat me as your enemy. Why are you so kind to me?'

'Your father was my truest friend,' answered David.

From then on Mephibosheth had an honoured place in David's palace and ate all his meals at the king's own table.

### Feasts and dancing in the streets

David wanted to please God, and looked for special ways to honour him. He decided to bring the precious box containing the laws of Moses into his new city. He ordered the priests to bring the box and he and his men marched in a splendid procession with them. David felt so happy he began to dance. He took off his royal robes and leaped and spun with all his might while his people watched, singing and playing their tambourines. His wife Michal saw

him. 'David's making a fool of himself, dancing like that in front of everyone,' she thought and she scolded him about it when he got home. But David didn't care. He knew that he had danced to praise God, and that God was pleased with him.

After the box was safely in Jerusalem David held a great feast. Everyone in the city received bread and cakes of dates and raisins to eat.

David was now a rich and powerful king. He built himself a palace in Jerusalem of trimmed stone and cedarwood and he lived there with his family.

Although he was busy governing the kingdom and building the city, he still tried to remember that it was only through God's help that he had become king. He would pick up his harp and sing songs about the ways God had helped him when his life had been in danger, and he had been alone and unhappy. We can still read in the Psalms in our Bibles the words David wrote so many centuries ago.

### David and Bathsheba

Although David tried to please
God, he sometimes disobeyed God
and brought trouble on himself.

Once, after he had been king
for some time, he fell in love
with a woman called Bathsheba
who was very beautiful. Like most
other kings of that time, David had
several wives, but although
Bathsheba was already married he
still wanted her for himself. Her
husband Uriah was one of his
soldiers, and this helped David to
think of a plan to get rid of him.
He sent a secret order to Uriah's
commanding officer, 'Place Uriah
in the front rank where the fighting
is fiercest. Then leave him on his
own so that he's sure to be killed.'

Before long the news came that
Uriah was dead, and almost
immediately David and Bathsheba
were married.

God was angry with David and
he sent a man called Nathan, a
holy man who loved and served
God, to show David how wrong he
had been. Nathan told David a
story.

'Once upon a time,' he began,
'two men lived in the same city.
One was rich, the other was poor.
The rich man had lots of sheep, the
poor man had only one little lamb,
which he treated like a pet – it
drank from his cup and liked to
nestle safely in his arms. One day
the rich man had an unexpected
visitor. He wanted to give his
friend a meal, but he was too mean
to kill one of his own sheep, so he
took the poor man's lamb and
killed it and ate that instead.'

This story made David very angry. 'The rich man deserves to die himself!' he exclaimed.

Nathan looked him between the eyes. '*You* are the rich man! You have done the same wicked thing by taking Uriah's wife from him and murdering Uriah!'

Then David saw how terribly he had acted. 'I have done wrong,' he said to Nathan. He was heart-broken and begged God to forgive him. God did forgive David, but from then on there was always trouble and quarrelling in David's large family.

In the course of time, however, Bathsheba had a baby boy, and in spite of all the trouble, she and David were delighted. They decided to call the child Solomon, which means 'peace'.

143

## KING SOLOMON

### Solomon's coronation

The years went by and King David grew old and had to stay in bed most of the time. Everyone wondered who would be the next king. They didn't know that David had chosen his son Solomon.

It should be me,' said Prince Adonijah, 'I'm David's eldest son. I should be the next king.'

He held a big feast and declared himself king, but he did not invite Solomon. As soon as Bathsheba heard about it she hurried to tell David.

'Your Majesty,' she said, bowing low. 'Remember, you once promised me that Solomon would be king in your place. Everyone in Israel is longing to know who's going to be king, and now your eldest son, Adonijah, is giving his friends a party and telling them all he's the next king.'

Nathan had heard what was going on, too. 'It's quite true,' he told David. 'They're all shouting, "Long live King Adonijah!" Of course they haven't invited any of us to their party.'

'But this is nonsense!' exclaimed David. 'Of course Solomon is to be king. You must have him anointed with oil at once.'

So Solomon and his friends left the palace in a solemn procession with Solomon riding on the king's mule out in front. One of the priests prayed and poured olive oil over Solomon's head, anointing him as king. The people who were watching blew their trumpets and shouted, 'Long live King Solomon!'

Prince Adonijah heard the cheering, too. He was terrified, but Solomon said, 'I won't kill Adonijah if he promises not to fight me.'

Adonijah came and bowed down to the new king. His plot had come to nothing.

## Solomon's dream

Before long David died of old age and Solomon had to rule by himself. He tried to do what God wanted and he would often pray to God for help. One night God spoke to him in a dream.

'What would you like me to give you?' God asked.

'You were always kind to my father David,' Solomon answered. 'He served you honestly and he loved you with all his heart. You've been kind to me, too, Lord, and made me king, but I'm still very young. I've never led men to battle as my father did, and you've put me in charge of the whole of Israel. I feel like a child, and I don't know how to manage.

'So, please, Lord, make me wise enough to be able to judge between what is right and what is wrong so that I can rule your people well.'

'You've chosen well,' said God. 'You might have asked for money and power for yourself, but you want to help others. Now I shall give you more than you asked. You shall be wiser than any other king, and I'll give you wealth and glory, too, but you must obey my laws as David your father did.'

Solomon woke up. He believed his dream was true and he offered sacrifices to thank God. Then he held a big party to celebrate God's promise.

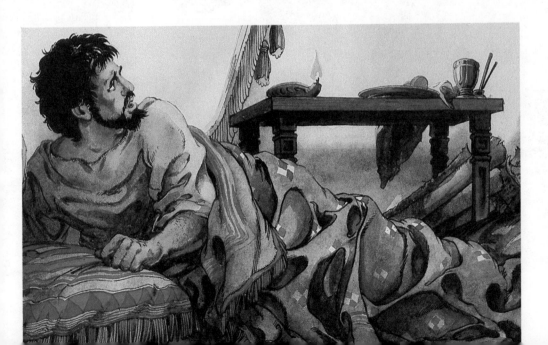

## A problem for Solomon

Soon Solomon became so famous for his wisdom that people brought their problems to him.

One day two women came to the palace. One of them carried a baby and they both looked very upset.

'Your Majesty,' one of the women explained. 'This woman and I both live in the same house. We've both just had babies, within three days of each other. The other night this woman's baby died. She got up and took my baby while I was asleep and left me her dead baby in its place.'

'No,' said the other woman, 'yours was the dead one.'

They started to argue in front of the king. How could Solomon discover which woman was telling the truth?

'Bring me a sword,' ordered Solomon. 'Now listen. I'll cut the baby in two and you can each have half.'

'All right,' agreed the second woman, but the first burst into tears.

'Oh, no, Sir, don't kill the baby. Let her have it.'

Solomon smiled, 'Now I know who the real mother is,' he said. 'She's the woman who wanted her child to live, even if she had to part with it. Here, take your baby home. I know you'll always be a good mother.'

The two women went home and everyone praised Solomon for settling their quarrel.

Solomon had been king for only four years when he started to work on a beautiful new building. It was to be a Temple where everyone could come and worship God, and Solomon built it in Jerusalem.

'Everything must be the very best for God's Temple,' Solomon thought. 'We must have white stone and carved wood and precious metal. My men know how to quarry stone and work with gold, but no one in Israel is really

skilful at working with wood. We will need help.'

So Solomon wrote to his father's friend King Hiram of Tyre, whose men were skilful woodmen. King Hiram was delighted to help. The forests of Lebanon, where tall cedar trees grew, belonged to him and he promised Solomon all the wood he needed.

'My men will choose the trees and cut them down for you,' he wrote to Solomon. 'Then they'll carry them to the sea and float them down the coast to Israel for your men to collect. All I ask in return is that you provide my men with food.' Solomon agreed gladly and the work began.

While Hiram's men worked in the forests of Lebanon, thousands of men from all over Israel were set to work in quarries, cutting blocks of limestone. Teams of oxen were used to haul them into place, and the building work began.

Right in the middle of the Temple the builders made a small, dark room, without any windows, and they lined it with gold. It was to hold their most treasured possession: the holy box which held the carved slabs of stone on which God's promises to Israel and his laws were written.

Outside the Temple was a courtyard where all the people could meet to worship God.

Here they built two great pillars of solid bronze, decorated like lilies. They gave them names, Jachin and Boaz. They also made a huge round bronze bowl shaped like a lily which they placed on the shining backs of twelve bulls made of bronze.

At last all the work was finished. 'It's taken seven whole years,' thought Solomon, 'but it's worth it!' He sent out a summons for every leader in Israel to come to Jerusalem for the special ceremony to bring the holy box to its new home inside the Temple.

They brought it into the courtyard and offered thousands of sacrifices as a special thank you to God. Then priests carried the box into the golden room at the heart of the Temple. Suddenly light, far more dazzling than the sunshine outside, filled the whole Temple.

It was as though God had come into the special little room they had set apart for him, and Solomon stretched out his hands to the sky.

'Oh, God, you made the sun and put it into the sky, yet you've allowed me to build you a special house where you can live among us for ever,' he prayed. 'When the people pray to you from this place, hear them in heaven where you live, and forgive them for all that they have done wrong.'

News of Solomon's wisdom and wealth spread far away. In the sunny land of Sheba the Queen herself heard about Solomon and decided to visit him. She travelled to Jerusalem on a camel, and with her came more camels all laden with gold and precious jewels and the wonderful spices for which Sheba was so famous.

'These are for you,' the Queen told Solomon, 'Now let me ask you some questions.'

'Tell me everything that's on your mind,' said Solomon. And to the Queen's delight he answered every single one of her questions that had been troubling her.

Perhaps he told her the proverbs for which he was famous. Here are some of them.

'A poor dinner eaten with people who love you is better than the juiciest meat if it's served with hatred.

Listen to your parents, because you wouldn't be here without them.

Remember, too, that a wise child makes his parents happy.

If you really want to be wise, obey God and learn his ways.'

Then Solomon showed the Queen the Temple and all his possessions. She saw the peacocks in his garden, the grapes and goblets of gold on his table, the jewels and beautiful clothes which he wore.

'I'd no idea you were so wise or so rich, Solomon!' she exclaimed. 'You've taken my breath away! I thank God that he has given Israel such a wise king.'

Solomon smiled. He gave orders for the Queen's camels to return with even more goods than they had brought, and the Queen rode away, still breathless with excitement at all she had heard and seen.

### Solomon's power and wealth

Solomon became still more powerful. Fleets of ships sailed across the sea carrying treasure for him. 'No king of Israel has had a navy before,' Solomon thought

proudly. 'My ships bring trade, and that makes me even richer. I watch them sail away and then come home again, even three years later, low in the water. Their holds are full of gold and ivory.

Peacocks spread their tails and scream as they strut across the decks and monkeys amuse the sailors with their antics,' he added, smiling to himself because he liked to watch the monkeys, too.

He didn't think of the men who left their families for three years and more to bring him his gold, nor of the ones who never returned from dangerous currents and stormy waves.

King David, Solomon's father, had hidden in caves and eaten the same food as his servants. Solomon ate rich food on golden plates and slept in a fine palace. Slaves and servants kept his chariots in good repair and looked after his horses in the huge stables he had built.

Even the Israelites who weren't Solomon's servants had to work for him. They were forced to leave their own jobs, their crops and their families and work on the building Solomon had ordered. Every three months they were marched away to work for one month without pay.

Only the men of Judah, Solomon's own tribe, were not forced to work for the king. The people began to complain.

'He makes us work like slaves in the very country God gave us for our own,' they grumbled. 'And he's married foreign wives, too. God told us not to do that, in case we started worshipping their gods, and that's just what Solomon's doing.'

Solomon had married foreign princesses so that their fathers would not fight him. However, his wives began to build shrines for their gods, and soon Solomon was tempted to worship foreign idols, too.

God was angry with Solomon. He warned him to stop praying to the gods and goddesses his wives worshipped, but Solomon did not obey him.

God was very angry with Solomon because he was disobedient. At last he said, 'You've broken your promise to me, Solomon, and disobeyed my commands. I shall take your kingdom from you, or at least, from your son. I won't take the whole kingdom away. Because I loved your father David who was true to me, and because I love Jerusalem which I have made my own city, the tribe of Judah will be left. But the other tribes will split off from your son's kingdom and be ruled by one of your servants, a man you've come to trust.'

It all happened as God said.

Solomon had once noticed how hard a young man called Jeroboam was working, repairing the walls round the eastern side of Jerusalem. He put him in charge of the men from two tribes who were being forced to work for the king and Jeroboam worked hard at his new job.

One day he had to leave Jerusalem. As he travelled along a lonely road he met a holy man called Ahijah. Ahijah was carrying a fine new cloak.

Suddenly he took it off and tore it into twelve long strips. He held

out ten pieces to Jeroboam.

'Just as I have torn up this cloak,' he said, 'God will divide Solomon's kingdom. Solomon's son shall rule over one tribe only. You, Jeroboam, shall rule over the rest.'

When Solomon heard what

Ahijah had said he tried to kill Jeroboam, but he escaped to Egypt.

After a few years Solomon died and his son became king. The ten tribes who had worked so hard for Solomon hoped that his son would treat them better.

Their leaders went to see him to ask him to rule them fairly and not to make them work like slaves as his father, Solomon, had done. Jeroboam came back from Egypt and joined them as they stood before the king.

At first the new king did not know what to say; some of his advisers told him to do as the people asked and some of them told him to treat them harshly in case they rebelled against him. At last he decided to be harsh.

'Listen,' he told the leader, 'my father made you work hard, but I shall make you work harder. He had you beaten like slaves, and I shall punish you even more severely!'

'Then we won't have you for our king!' shouted the people. 'You can mine your own copper and dig your own limestone. We're going home!'

Solomon's son had to escape quickly to Jerusalem or the people would have killed him; only two tribes remained loyal to him. The ten tribes whose leaders he had threatened so cruelly made Jeroboam their king. The country was split in two.

# ELIJAH AND ELISHA

## Elijah warns King Ahab

Now Jeroboam was the ruler of the northern tribes. He wanted to make sure that his people did not go back to Jerusalem to worship God in the Temple in case they decided to join the kingdom of Judah again, so he set up two golden statues in his own territory.

'Now you can pray to your own gods here in Israel,' he told his people. 'You don't need to go to Jerusalem any more.'

After Jeroboam's death one bad king followed another, and things went from bad to worse in Israel. At last, in the reign of a king called Ahab, it seemed as though no one in the whole kingdom loved God any more. Or so one man thought sadly. His name was Elijah, and he was a man who tried to serve God faithfully and worship him properly. He longed for his country to have a good king who would obey God.

'King Ahab doesn't obey God,' he thought. 'He has even built a temple for the foreign god, Baal, that his wife, Queen Jezebel, worships. Everyone prays there now! As if a statue could help them! Only God can do that. I'm going to tell King Ahab that he must mend his ways!'

Barefoot and dressed in rough skins, with a stern expression on his face, Elijah strode off over the hills. Grey clouds hid the sun. The rainy season was about to begin.

Elijah walked all the way to King Ahab's fine palace with its richly carved furniture and its floors set with ivory.

The king and queen stared at him in surprise as he strode boldly into their room. Elijah spoke to the king in a voice like thunder.

'I've heard how you tried to kill everyone who won't worship your wife's god, Baal,' he said. 'But I still serve God, and I've come to tell you that God, not Baal, is in control. And as proof of what I say, there won't be any more rain, not even a dew drop, until God says so!'

He turned and walked away, his bare feet padding softly over the beautiful floor, and the king and queen stared after him in fury.

They decided to kill him but Elijah went quickly into hiding.

God told Elijah to go to a valley near the River Jordan where he would be safe. A brook called Cherith ran through the valley so Elijah had plenty of water. But he needed food, too and nothing grew on the bare hills around him.

'I'll send some ravens with food for you,' said God. Every morning and evening ravens flew into the valley carrying bread and meat for Elijah in their beaks. He always had enough to eat, but before long the brook began to stop chattering over its stony bed. It was drying up, for there had been no rain to fill it, just as Elijah had said. Soon there was only a trickle of water, and at last no water at all.

'Now perhaps the king will believe in God and stop worshipping Baal,' thought Elijah, 'but I shall die here with nothing to drink.'

'Leave the valley now,' said God. 'Go to the coast. You'll find a new friend there who will look after you.'

### Elijah meets a poor woman

It was a long journey. The ground was so hard and dry that all the crops had withered. Elijah felt hungry and thirsty when at last he arrived at a small village near the sea.

A poor woman came along gathering sticks.

'Please could you bring me a drink of water?' Elijah asked. As the woman turned away to fetch some water he called after her, 'Could you bring me a piece of bread, too? I'm so hungry.'

The woman stopped. She was almost as poorly dressed as Elijah, and he could tell that it was a long time since she had eaten a proper meal.

'I've not a scrap of food in the house,' she said. 'And that's the truth. All I've got is a handful of flour in the bottom of my barrel and a drop of oil. I'm gathering sticks to light a fire so that I can bake a pancake for my little son and myself. That's all we've got to eat and then we'll have to starve.'

'Don't be afraid,' Elijah said. 'Go and make your pancake but make me a small scone first, please. God will look after you and your son until it starts to rain and there'll always be flour in your barrel and oil in your jar.'

The woman hurried home. Soon she rushed back to Elijah. 'Here's your scone, sir! And it's true! My barrel's full of flour. Come and stay in our house now.' So Elijah stayed in the woman's house and there was always enough to eat even though it didn't rain at all.

### Contest on Mount Carmel

Three years went by before God said to Elijah, 'Go and tell King Ahab that I'm going to let it rain.'

So Elijah told Ahab to call together the priests of Baal and all the people to a mountain called Mount Carmel.

'We'll have a contest to see who the real God is,' Elijah told the priests.

Once everyone had arrived Elijah told them to build an altar to Baal. They built an altar, piled firewood high on top of it and heaved a bull on top to burn as an offering to their god.

'Wait a minute. Don't light the fire yet,' called Elijah. 'Pray to Baal. If he's a real god he'll send fire to burn up the bull!'

All day the priests and people prayed to Baal, but not a spark fell out of the sky to kindle their fire. Elijah watched and laughed at them.

'Shout louder,' he told them. 'Perhaps Baal has gone on a journey, or maybe he's asleep.'

Finally he told them to stop. 'It's my turn to build my altar now,' he said. 'But I want you to pour water over my firewood until it's too wet to burn. Then we'll see who is more powerful, God or Baal.'

Then Elijah prayed to God, 'Lord, prove now that you really are the God of Israel. Answer my prayer so that everyone will believe in you.'

Immediately the sodden wood on Elijah's altar began to hiss. A flame spurted high. The wood crackled as the fire blazed. Even the stones were burnt. Everyone bowed to the ground chanting, 'The Lord really is God.'

Then they killed the priests who had led them to worship Baal and Elijah turned to the king. 'Go and eat now, King Ahab. I can hear the rush and roar of a great rainstorm.'

But the sky was still blue and there wasn't a cloud to be seen. King Ahab sat down and ate a meal while the people scattered to their homes. But Elijah climbed to the top of Mount Carmel, taking a servant with him. He knelt and prayed, his face bowed down on the earth.

'Now have a look towards the sea,' he told his servant.

The servant scanned the horizon. 'There's not a cloud in the sky,' he called.

'Look again,' said Elijah. 'Look seven times.'
The seventh time
the servant yelled,
'There's a small

cloud no bigger than my hand blowing up from the sea.'

'Then run and tell King Ahab to drive off home before he gets soaked,' called Elijah.

The sky grew dark and the wind howled over the mountain tops, driving storm-clouds across the sky. A few drops of rain spattered the earth. The king jumped into his chariot. He urged the horses on as fast as

he could, but now God gave Elijah such strength that he went racing down the mountain faster than the chariot and ran on through the downpour ahead of the king.

When the queen heard that Elijah had killed all the priests who served Baal she was furious and sent him a message. 'By this time tomorrow you'll be a dead man!'

### God speaks to Elijah

Elijah fled for his life. He ran into the desert until he could go no further. Finally, he hid under a juniper bush.

He was so tired and hungry that he quite forgot that God had helped him to win a great victory over all the priests of Baal. 'I can't go on any more,' he groaned. 'Let me die, Lord.' He was so tired he fell asleep.

Suddenly he felt someone touch him and he started up in alarm. An angel stood in front of him. 'Get up and have something to eat, Elijah,' said the angel.

Elijah sniffed. There was a good smell in the air. A loaf was baking on the hot stones close by, and a jug of water stood beside it. Elijah had some bread to eat and went back to sleep. The angel woke him again. 'Eat and drink, Elijah. You've a long journey ahead and you need food.'

Elijah finished the bread and travelled on through the desert. It took him forty more days to reach the holy mountain where long ago God had given Moses and the people their Law.

It was getting dark and Elijah took shelter in a cave. There God spoke to him. 'What are you doing here, Elijah?' God asked.

'I'm distressed because I'm your only faithful follower,' said Elijah. 'And now they are trying to kill me.'

'Go and stand outside,' God replied.

Then God sent a wind tearing over the mountain. Rocks rattled down the slopes and the storm seemed to be blowing the mountain apart. Elijah watched for God, but God was not in the storm.

Then the wind dropped and the ground began to shudder. An earthquake made the ground rumble and shake under Elijah's feet, but God was not in the earthquake.

The shaking stopped. Flames leapt among the rocks and fire crackled through the long dry grass. Elijah shaded his face from the heat and the glare, but he did not see God in the fire.

Then everything became very still and God spoke in the quietness. Elijah covered his face with his cloak and went out of the cave as God had told him to.

'Don't think you're the only one in Israel to follow me,' came God's voice. 'I have seven thousand other true followers who don't worship Baal at all. I can make even kings carry out my plans. But I know how lonely you feel, Elijah, and I am giving you a friend, a man called Elisha. Go and find him. He'll help you now and carry on your work some day when you have gone.'

## A new helper for Elijah

Elijah set off in search of Elisha and found him with eleven friends, ploughing, each man guiding two oxen yoked to a wooden plough. As Elisha came by, Elijah reached out and tossed his cloak across Elisha's shoulders.

Elisha understood. He left his plough and ran up to Elijah. 'I'll be your helper but let me go and say goodbye to my family,' he said.

'Of course,' Elijah agreed.

Elisha hurried back to his plough. He killed his oxen and chopped up their yoke and the plough for firewood. He roasted the oxen and shared a good-bye meal with his family and friends. Then he walked away with Elijah.

Elijah and Elisha worked together teaching people about God, and King Ahab and his wife never managed to stop them.

At last the time came when Elijah knew that God was going to take him away.

He didn't say anything, but Elisha knew that something unusual was going to happen.

The two friends walked to the banks of the River Jordan. Then Elijah hit the water hard with his cloak and a path appeared for them to walk across.

'Ask me one last thing,' Elijah said.

'Leave me a double share of your power to help me carry on your work,' Elisha replied.

'That's hard,' said Elijah. 'But it will be yours if you see God carry me away.'

They walked on. Suddenly a splendid fiery chariot pulled by flaming horses flashed between them and whirled Elijah away.

But Elisha saw him disappear and he cried, 'My father, the chariots and horsemen of Israel!'

He tore at his clothes and wept in grief. Then he noticed Elijah's cloak on the ground. Elisha picked it up and went back to the Jordan.

'Help me, God, as you helped Elijah,' he prayed and hit the river with the cloak. The water swished back as it had done before and a startled crowd on the other bank watched Elisha walk across the river. They all came and bowed before him.

### The rich woman's son comes back to life

Elisha travelled about the country with his servant Gehazi. There was a rich woman who invited him for a meal whenever he came to her village.

'Elisha's one of God's servants,' she told her husband. 'Let's make him a spare room on the roof so that he can rest here whenever he comes by.'

Elisha was very grateful and wanted to do something for her in return.

'She would like a baby,' Gehazi said. 'She and her husband have no children.'

So Elisha told her that God would give them a baby and to her delight she had a son.

A few years later the little boy went out to watch the harvesters at work in the fields. The sun was very hot and he suddenly clutched his head.

'Father, help me, I've got such a headache!' he cried.

A servant took him home to his mother and he died in her arms. She carried him to the spare room and laid him on Elisha's bed.

Then she saddled a donkey and rode away to find Elisha, who came back at once. He went into the spare room and shut the door. First he prayed and then he stretched himself on top of the child, pressing his face against the boy's face until the cold body grew warm. Suddenly the boy sneezed seven times and opened his eyes.

His mother was overjoyed. She bowed to the ground, thanking Elisha and then carried her child back downstairs to tell everyone the good news.

Elisha helped people whenever he could and because he trusted God he could often do very wonderful things.

### Elisha and the poisoned stew

Once while Elisha was teaching a group of very poor people about God, Gehazi his servant started to cook their dinner. Food was very scarce and they hunted for herbs and berries to make their stew go further. One man found a wild vine laden with fruit.

'I don't know what this is, but there is so much fruit it will help to fill us up,' he thought. He picked as much fruit as he could carry back with him, chopped it up and put it all in the pot.

But the fruit was poisonous.

'We'll die if we eat this,' the men cried when they tasted the stew. 'It's poisoned. What can we do?' they asked Elisha. 'There's nothing else to eat.'

'Don't worry,' Elisha said. He picked up some flour and added it to the cooking pot. 'It's quite safe now,' he assured them, so they all enjoyed the rest of their meal and no one came to any harm.

Some time afterwards a famous army commander from another country, Syria, came to Elisha for help.

The commander was called Naaman. He won a battle against Israel and among his prisoners was a little girl. He took her home to his wife to be her servant.

One day Naaman's wife told the girl some sad news. 'Naaman is ill. He's got leprosy. No one can make him better and he'll have to go away and live all by himself in case anyone else catches it.'

'I wish he'd go back to Israel,' said the servant girl at once. 'Elisha could make him better, I'm sure.'

So Naaman asked the king of Syria if he could go off to Israel. 'Of course,' the king agreed. 'I'll send a letter to the king of Israel. Go straight to him. I'll tell him he must cure you.'

Full of hope Naaman set out, taking silver and gold and fine clothing as presents for the person who would make him better.

But the king of Israel tore his clothes in dismay when he heard what Naaman wanted. 'This must be a trick! The king of Syria is trying to start a fight! Of course I can't cure anyone.'

But Elisha sent the king a message. 'Send Naaman to me. I'll show him that God is still at work in Israel.'

So Naaman rode off to Elisha's house. Elisha didn't even come out to meet him. He sent Gehazi instead.

'My master says you must go and wash seven times in the River Jordan and you'll be cured,' said Gehazi.

Naaman was furious. 'I haven't come all this way to be told to go and have a wash!' he exclaimed. 'Besides we've got two fine rivers at home. Why can't I wash there instead of in this muddy river?' And he rode away in a temper.

But his servants begged him, 'Sir, please do what Elisha wants. After all, if he'd asked you to do something difficult you would have tried it at once.'

Naaman calmed down. He waded into the River Jordan and dipped under seven times and

washed himself. When he came out every trace of leprosy had gone and his skin was smooth and soft, just like a little child's.

Naaman rode back to thank Elisha and give him the presents he had brought, but Elisha would accept nothing.

'Well then, just let me tell you, sir, that I believe in your God now and I'll never pray to any other god again,' declared Naaman.

Elisha smiled. 'Go home in peace,' he said.

So Naaman went home to his wife and her servant girl and Elisha went on with his work for God.

Elisha helped many people and taught them about God, but after his death people forgot what he had taught them. No enemies came to attack them, they had fine houses to live in and plenty of good things to eat and drink. They were comfortable, and they did not want to bother with God. They broke his laws, they cheated one another and lied.

At last, some seventy years after Elisha's death, powerful armies from a country called Assyria did come to attack them. The people were soft and lazy because of their comfortable life, and they were too proud to admit that they had done wrong and ask God for his help.

The Assyrians conquered the country easily, and took the people away as prisoners.

# JEREMIAH

## God's special messenger

While all these things were happening in the northern kingdom, the little kingdom of Judah was having its own problems. More than two hundred years had passed since the kingdom of Judah broke away from King Jeroboam. Good kings and bad kings followed one another and in the end the Assyrians marched against Judah, too. However, a good king, called Hezekiah, was ruling at that time, and with God's help he was able to save his people from the enemy. After Hezekiah's death, though, a wicked king came to the throne. He ruled for many years, and he turned right away from God. He set up statues to other gods in Jerusalem, and even killed his own son as a sacrifice to them. Before long many of the people of Judah had given up worshipping God and started worshipping these false gods, too. The people of Judah were becoming as bad as the people of Israel. At last God decided to send a special messenger to them. He wanted to warn them to come back to him before it was too late, or he would leave them as he had left the people of Israel.

The man whom God chose for this job was called Jeremiah. He lived in a quiet village in the country and he was still quite a young man when God spoke to him.

'What do you see, Jeremiah?' he heard God's voice asking him.

'I see an almond tree in early bloom,' replied Jeremiah.

'I am like the almond tree, Jeremiah,' God said, 'for I too am early; early to warn my people. My people have disobeyed me, and I want you to tell them to turn back to me. Remind them of what I've done for them and warn them to stop their wicked ways or their enemies will come and destroy them.'

'But, Lord, I'm still so young,' Jeremiah answered in alarm. 'Who's going to listen to me?' He was really frightened!

'Don't be afraid,' God replied. 'I chose you to be my messenger, before you were born. I shall go with you and help you. You will be speaking my words, not your own.'

## Jeremiah is laughed at

So Jeremiah said goodbye to his family and friends in the quiet village where the almond trees grew and set off for Jerusalem. He went off to the Temple and stood on the steps to deliver God's message:

'You have forgotten God over and over again, but those gods you worship won't help you when our enemies send powerful armies marching against us,' Jeremiah warned. But the passers-by only laughed and made fun of him.

'You're wrong to laugh,' Jeremiah answered, 'just as you're wrong to listen to the false messengers who tell you that everything's going to be easy and peaceful. I can feel God's anger burning inside me, and my heart is sad for you. I wish there were some way of helping you. I'm so sorry for you I could cry all day and all night. Strong armies are going to capture this beautiful city and take you all prisoner. God won't stop them, because you won't turn back to him.'

177

But still the people laughed and refused to listen to Jeremiah's words. So Jeremiah tried to show them something that would help them to understand. He went along to the workshop where the potter turned clay on a wheel to make plates and jugs, dishes and oil lamps.

The potter looked upset. 'There's something wrong,' he exclaimed. 'Look, this lump of clay on the wheel has gone out of shape.'

He stopped the wheel, pulled off the clay that had gone wrong and found a little stone inside it. 'Now I'll start again,' he said. 'It's

178

important to get it right.' Quite a crowd had gathered to watch the potter at work.

'God is like the potter,' said Jeremiah, 'and we're like the clay. Our disobedience is just like that stone which spoilt the clay, and God is going to have to take it away, even if it means destroying Jerusalem.'

But still no one believed him.

Jeremiah tried to show them even more clearly what he meant. One day he bought a large clay pot and showed it to some of the priests and leaders.

'Come with me to that dreadful valley just outside Jerusalem where people have been offering sacrifices to foreign gods,' he told them.

They all followed Jeremiah out to the valley. He held the jar high above his head.

'Look at me and listen well to what God says,' he cried. 'You have disobeyed God and worshipped foreign gods in this very place. You've even killed your own children and burnt them here as offerings to statues who can never hear your prayers or help you. And that is something that God has told us never to do.

'Well then, God is warning us that enemies will surround our city and we'll starve inside our own walls. Watch this!' He hurled the heavy clay jar to the ground. It crashed to the earth and broke into pieces.

'Jerusalem and all its people will be like this broken pot,' explained Jeremiah, 'God will let our enemies break us completely.'

### Jeremiah is arrested

Now the priests and other leaders liked to tell the people that Jerusalem was safe and would never be attacked. They hated Jeremiah for what he said, and one of the priests, called Pashur, had him arrested.

'I'm going to punish you because you keep telling everyone that powerful armies will destroy us. What kind of message is that, you traitor!' Pashur said angrily.

He had Jeremiah beaten and chained up outside the Temple where everyone could see him. He had to stay there on the hard pavement all night long. His enemies stood round and laughed at him. They thought he would keep quiet now, but nothing could stop Jeremiah. God's words throbbed on his lips and he had to speak them. He even had a special message for Pashur next morning when he came to set him free.

'You'll see your friends murdered, Pashur,' he warned. 'Then you'll remember God's message which you refuse to believe now. You see, our enemies will certainly defeat us. They'll destroy Jerusalem, and Pashur, you'll be captured and taken away for ever.'

Pashur unlocked his chains silently and Jeremiah stumbled stiffly away.

'Oh, God, your words burn like fire inside me,' he groaned. 'I have to go on speaking, even if no one believes.'

### Jeremiah won't give up

In the end the priests forbade Jeremiah to go into the Temple and speak God's message, but he was determined that people should

still hear the warnings that God gave them to turn back to him. So he asked his friend, Baruch, to write down for him on long scrolls of parchment the words which he dictated.

'Now you can go into the Temple and read out God's words from the scroll,' said Jeremiah. 'The people will hear God's message even though I'm not allowed to speak to them myself.'

So Baruch went to the Temple and started to read aloud from the scroll.

The king's officials overheard him. 'Did Jeremiah tell you what to write?' they demanded.

'Yes he did,' admitted Baruch, and he hurried to warn Jeremiah. The officials took his scroll to the king, who ordered one of his secretaries to read it to him.

The words on the scroll made the king very angry because, like the other leaders, he refused to listen to God and kept telling the people that their enemy, the king of Babylon, wouldn't really defeat them.

He seized hold of a knife. 'Keep reading,' he told his secretary. Every time the man reached the end of a column of writing the king slashed the scroll. Long curling strips fell on the floor and the king stuffed them into the small fire which burnt in the room because it was winter.

'If the people heard all this they'd surrender to the enemy!' the king declared. 'Jeremiah's a traitor!'

He tried to have him arrested, but Jeremiah had managed to hide away safely.

Jeremiah was still determined.

'God's words are stronger than the king's,' he said. 'Come on, Baruch, sharpen your pen, and get your ink ready, because we must write those words down all over again. God will help us to remember them.'

So Baruch set to work and wrote God's message down once more. Some of the people began to believe God's words, but the king and his leaders refused to listen to them.

### The siege of Jerusalem

Then the king died and his son ruled instead. The new king was wiser than his father, and when the king of Babylon finally surrounded Jerusalem with his armies and they attacked its strong walls with their battering rams the new king realised he wasn't strong enough to fight back. He gave himself up and was marched away to Babylon along with other leaders and the best craftsmen and most skilled workers. The king of Babylon chose another king called Zedekiah to reign over the people left in Jerusalem, but Zedekiah was a weak man and a foolish king. He kept trying to rebel against the king of Babylon and Jeremiah knew that he was wrong and that he was putting the people in danger.

Sometimes God spoke to Jeremiah by showing him pictures. Once he showed him two baskets of figs. One basket was full of good ripe figs, but the other held shrivelled bad figs which weren't fit to eat.

'Jeremiah,' said God, 'I want you to understand that all the people who gave themselves up to the king of Babylon and were marched away are like the good figs in that basket. It doesn't matter that they are far away in a foreign place. I will see that they are treated kindly. I will fill their hearts with such longing for me that they will turn back to me and love me. But King Zedekiah and his foolish advisers and everyone who refused to listen to me and have stayed behind in Jerusalem are like the bad figs. One day they'll be destroyed by their enemies, because they're just like these bad figs and they're only fit to be tipped out and destroyed.'

Of course, as soon as King Zedekiah tried to rebel against the Babylonians they came back and besieged Jerusalem just as Jeremiah had warned. Nobody could get in or out of the city. Then one day the Babylonians heard that the Egyptians were marching against them. Leaving Jerusalem they attacked the Egyptian army, and so for a short

They took Jeremiah and locked him in a dungeon deep underground and there he stayed for a long time. By now the Babylonian armies had come back and King Zedekiah was frightened. He called Jeremiah from his cell to ask him if God had any message to help him.

'The message is the same as it's always been,' said Jeremiah. 'You

time the Jews were free to move about again.

At this time Jeremiah decided to visit the little village where he had spent his childhood. He got ready to leave the city. This was the chance his enemies were waiting for. They lay in wait for him, and as he reached the city gate they arrested him.

'You're nothing but a spy,' they accused him. 'Look, we've caught you on your way to join our enemies!'

know God wants you to turn back to him and agree to serve the king of Babylon whose armies are far too strong for us to fight. Now, please tell me, Your Majesty, what crime I've committed to be locked up like this. I've always spoken the truth and I'll die if I'm sent back to that underground cell.'

King Zedekiah wouldn't listen to Jeremiah's message, but he did let him out of prison. Now he was kept chained in the palace courtyard.

While he was in the courtyard Jeremiah went on telling everyone to listen to God. 'If you keep on trying to fight against the

Babylonian armies you'll starve to death,' he warned. 'They won't let you into the city. Besides, it's only a matter of time before they capture us.'

Pashur, the priest, Jeremiah's old enemy, overheard.

'Put Jeremiah to death,' he urged King Zedekiah. 'He's making everyone more afraid than ever with these messages of his. You must stop him talking!'

'Go ahead then, do what you think is best,' agreed the king weakly.

Pashur and some others tied a rope round Jeremiah and lowered him into a deep pit. It had once been used as a well, but there was no water left, only mud. Jeremiah sank down into the slime. He knew he would die there without food or water but he did not despair because he still trusted God. And in fact God was about to rescue him.

One of the king's officials heard what had happened and hurried to the king. His name was Ebed-Melech and he came from Ethiopia in Africa. He asked permission to rescue Jeremiah, and Zedekiah agreed. Ebed-Melech fetched strong ropes and rushed to the old well.

'Jeremiah!' he called. 'Tie this rope round you. Here are some rags. Put them under your armpits so that the rope won't hurt. Ready? Right! I'll pull as hard as I can.'

Slowly he pulled Jeremiah out of the well into the light of day. After that Jeremiah was kept in the palace courtyard again, and although the priests hoped he might have learned his lesson he went on trying to persuade everyone to believe God's words.

### Jeremiah buys a field

One day Jeremiah did a strange thing. Although he was stuck in Jerusalem he bought a field near his old village. A crowd gathered in the palace courtyard to watch him sign two pieces of parchment as proof that the field was now his property. He put the parchments into a clay pot.

'Now, listen, everyone,' he said. 'The walls of Jerusalem will soon be battered down. The Babylonians will come in and burn down the houses where people have worshipped statues instead of

God. They'll destroy the city. So why do you think I'm buying a field when soon we'll all be marched away as prisoners? Well, I want you to understand that one day God will bring back to this country those people who will love and serve him faithfully and not pray to other gods as you have done. Then there will be a time of peace and happiness and everyone will live safely in their own homes and plough their own fields.'

It wasn't long after this that Jerusalem's strong walls gave way and the armies of Babylon stormed the city. King Zedekiah and his soldiers tried to escape but they were captured and taken in chains to Babylon.

### Jeremiah's last journey

Jeremiah himself was set free, but decided to stay with the poor people who weren't rich or important enough to be considered dangerous and had been left behind in Jerusalem by the Babylonians. But in the end these people, too, rebelled against the Babylonians, and the governor whom the king of Babylon had left to rule Jerusalem was murdered. The people who were responsible were frightened and they decided to escape to Egypt.

First of all, however, they decided to ask Jeremiah's advice. They said they wanted to know what God would want them to do. Jeremiah warned them not to go.

'You won't escape the king of Babylon in Egypt,' he told them. 'Stay here and serve God.' But although the people had asked Jeremiah for advice they refused to listen. They even made Jeremiah go to Egypt with them. He left Jerusalem sadly, knowing that he would never see his own country again. In Egypt he went on urging his people to turn back to God, until at last he died.

Jeremiah's words brought him trouble all his life. He was always lonely – he never married and had children, and his messages turned everyone against him. But Jeremiah never stopped believing that God was with him, helping him, and telling him what to say. In the end Jeremiah's messages began to help the people to realise how much God loved them. They were written down, and after Jeremiah's death, when the Jews had begun to love God and follow him again, they turned to Jeremiah's words and began to understand them at last.

# DANIEL AND ESTHER

## *A special diet*

The Jewish people who were taken away from their homeland to Babylon turned back to God and tried to follow his ways exactly as God had told Jeremiah. However, they had very many difficulties to face in their new country.

When the Jewish captives arrived in Babylon, King Nebuchadnezzar ordered the official in charge of his household to choose some of the young prisoners to serve in the court. 'Teach them our language and train them in our ways,' he said, 'and let them eat the food from the royal tables.'

So the official chose several young men, including a handsome young prince called Daniel and his three friends Shadrach, Meshach and Abednego.

At first Daniel and his friends were pleased, but there was one problem. 'We can't eat Babylonian food,' Daniel told the official. 'The God we serve has given us rules about the kinds of things we may eat. We would break them if we ate your meals.'

The official was alarmed. 'If you get thin they'll cut off my head,' he said. So Daniel asked one of the guards for help.

'You can test us,' he said boldly. 'Give us vegetables and water for ten days, and then see if we look fit or not.'

The guard agreed. Ten days later the four young men looked fitter and healthier than the others who had been eating the king's food.

'All right, you can stay on your diet!' the guard told them. God had helped Daniel and his friends to obey him.

## Nebuchadnezzar's dream

Nebuchadnezzar had a dream soon afterwards, which bothered him so much that he ordered his magicians to tell him the meaning – but he refused to tell them what the dream was.

'I expect you magicians to explain my dream whether you know what the dream is or not,' he said.

'That's impossible,' stammered the magicians.

'Then I'll have you all put to death, even Daniel and his friends,' said the king.

When Daniel heard the news he rushed off to tell his friends.

'Let's pray that God will show us the meaning of the king's dream,' he suggested.

That very night God showed Daniel what the dream was and what it meant. Daniel hurried to the king.

'God has shown me what your dream was all about,' he told Nebuchadnezzar. 'You saw a giant statue gleaming with gold and silver. As you watched, a stone fell on the statue and broke it into pieces. Then the stone grew into a mountain that covered the whole earth. The dream is to show you that although human kings may be as powerful as that statue, God is even more powerful. One day he will send his own king to set up a kingdom that will never end.'

Nebuchadnezzar was very impressed. 'Your God is more powerful than any other,' he said. 'I'm going to put you in charge of all my advisers.'

## Into the furnace

Some time later Nebuchadnezzar had a huge gold statue made, which everyone had to worship. 'Every time you hear the musicians playing their instruments: the trumpet, flute, harp, oboe, zither or any other instrument, you must fall down before this statue and worship it,' he ordered. 'Anyone who refuses will be thrown into a blazing furnace.'

All over Babylon everyone did as the king ordered, everyone except Daniel's friends, Shadrach, Meshach and Abednego. Nebuchadnezzar called them before him. 'What's this?' he demanded. 'I'll throw you into that furnace if you don't worship my statue. Not even your God will be able to rescue you.'

'We serve the true God, your Majesty,' answered Shadrach, Meshach and Abednego. 'Perhaps he'll rescue us, but even if he doesn't, we're not going to worship your statue.'

'Make the furnace seven times hotter,' yelled Nebuchadnezzar. 'Tie up these men and throw them into the flames.'

The blaze was so hot it burnt the soldiers who pushed Shadrach, Meshach and Abednego into the furnace. The three friends toppled forward into the fire.

Suddenly Nebuchadnezzar jumped to his feet. 'Look!' he shouted. 'Didn't we throw three people into the furnace? Well, now there are four people walking about completely unharmed, right in the middle of the flames! And the fourth one is so splendid he must be an angel.' He went to the furnace door and called, 'Shadrach, Meshach and Abednego, come out!'

The three friends walked calmly out of the blazing furnace, completely unhurt. The fire hadn't singed so much as a hair and even their clothes had no smell of burning. 'God sent his angel to save you!' declared Nebuchadnezzar. 'You risked your life rather than disobey him. From now on no one is ever to speak disrespectfully of you or your God.'

### Daniel and the lions

Many years passed. Nebuchadnezzar died and a new king called Darius came to the throne. He soon decided that Daniel, who was now an old man, was so honest and trustworthy that he wanted to put him in charge of all his officials just as Nebuchadnezzar had done. That made the other officials jealous of Daniel. They thought of a plan to have him killed. 'Please sign this law,' they said to Darius. The law decreed that no one was to pray to any God except to King Darius himself for one whole month. Whoever did was to be thrown into a pit where lions were kept. Darius signed the law and the officials went away to spy on Daniel.

'The king can't change the law now he's signed it,' they muttered. 'He'll have to throw Daniel to the lions because that man will never pray to anyone except his God.' They were right. Daniel still knelt down by his window which faced towards his homeland far away and prayed there, quite openly, three times a day, just as he always did.

The officials lost no time. They reported Daniel to the king who had to obey his own law, even though he respected Daniel more than all his other advisers. So Daniel was flung into the pit where lions prowled. The king sealed the entrance. There was no escape.

'Only your God can save you now,' the king cried, and he was so upset he lay awake all night, thinking of Daniel. As soon as it was light he hurried to the pit.

'Daniel, was your God really able to save you from the lions?' he called anxiously.

To his joy he heard Daniel's voice. 'Long live your Majesty! God sent his angel and shut the lions' mouths. They haven't hurt me at all.'

The king had Daniel pulled out of the pit at once. 'Now everyone in my vast empire must respect your God who does such wonderful things!' he declared. Daniel stayed faithful to God till the end of his life.

## Esther is made queen

Many years went by. Daniel and the people who had come to Babylon with him as prisoners all died, but their children and grandchildren still lived in Babylon.

Among them was a young Jewish girl called Esther. She was an orphan and she lived with her cousin Mordecai, who had brought her up.

The king of Babylon at that time was called Xerxes. One day he decided he wanted a new queen. He ordered all the most beautiful girls in the kingdom to come to his palace at Susa, so that he could choose the one he liked best to be his wife. Now Esther was very beautiful so she was taken to the palace with the other girls. Mordecai warned her to tell no one where she came from. For a whole year Esther and the other girls lived in the women's quarters of the palace and were given special beauty treatments before the king saw them. No one in the palace knew that Esther was Jewish or that Mordecai was her cousin.

When it was Esther's turn to go before the king she looked so beautiful that Xerxes fell in love with her at once. 'You are the wife I have been looking for!' he exclaimed. 'You shall be my queen!'

He put the royal crown on Esther's head and that night he held a great feast in her honour. Everyone in the kingdom had a holiday to celebrate the wedding.

## Plots in the palace

Mordecai had a job in the palace, but still no one knew that he was the queen's cousin! One day, he overheard two of the king's guards plotting to murder the king.

I must find Esther and get her to warn the king, he thought. When Esther heard Mordecai's tale, she hurried to warn the king who had the two guards arrested and hanged.

'Make sure that all this is noted down in the palace records,' ordered the king. 'Mordecai has saved my life.'

However, although all the details were written down, nothing was done to reward Mordecai. The king had just appointed a new prime minister, and everyone was too busy attending to him to remember what Mordecai had done.

The new prime minister was called Haman. Xerxes was very pleased with him, and he ordered all his other officials to bow to the ground in front of Haman whenever they saw him. Only Mordecai refused.

'I'm a Jew,' he explained to the other officials. 'I only bow in worship to God.' Haman was so furious he went to the king.

'Your Majesty,' he said, 'in your

He put on pieces of rough cloth and covered his head with ashes as a sign of grief. Then he walked through the streets to the palace with tears streaming down his face.

Queen Esther sent a trusted servant out to speak to Mordecai to find out why he was so upset.

Mordecai told the servant what the king had done. 'Ask Esther to beg Xerxes for mercy,' he added.

'Oh, dear, that won't be easy at

empire there are people called Jews who refuse to obey your orders. They should all be executed.'

Xerxes agreed and he sent messengers throughout the empire to say that on the thirteenth day of that very month every single Jew, man, woman and child was to be killed. When Mordecai heard the news he tore his clothes to shreds.

all,' exclaimed Esther in dismay. 'Anyone who even enters the king's rooms without his permission can be put to death. It's a whole month since the king last spoke to me. I've only got one hope. If the king holds out his golden sceptre when he sees me, I'll know that he's feeling merciful and I'll be able to speak to him.'

On the third day Esther put on her royal robes and went to the king. She waited in the hall facing the throne and the king looked up. To Esther's relief he held out the golden sceptre as soon as he saw her.

'What can I do for you?' he asked as Esther touched the sceptre.

'Will you and Haman come and have dinner with me tonight?' Esther asked, for she had a plan.

The king and Haman dined with Esther that night, and then the king asked Esther again what he could do for her. 'Come and dine with me tomorrow too, and I shall tell you then,' Esther replied.

Haman was delighted to have a second invitation from Queen Esther, but as he left the palace he saw Mordecai, and, as usual, Mordecai wouldn't bow down to him.

'How I hate that man!' Haman exclaimed. 'I won't enjoy my power until he's dead!'

### Esther risks her life

Bravely Esther decided to take the risk for the sake of her people. She sent an urgent message back to Mordecai. 'Gather all the Jews in Susa together and spend the next three days praying for me. Don't eat or drink anything. Just pray, and my maids and I will do the same. Then I'll go to the king and if he puts me to death, well, I shall just have to die.'

### Mordecai is rewarded

That night Xerxes couldn't sleep, so to pass the time till daylight he ordered a servant to read the palace records aloud to him. When he reached the report about the plot that Mordecai had discovered, Xerxes remembered that he had never rewarded him. So he called for Haman and said to

202

him, 'There's someone I want to reward. What do you suggest?'

'The king must mean me!' thought Haman, so he said, 'Order one of your most important noblemen to dress the man in royal robes and lead him on horseback through the city announcing that this is how your Majesty treats someone you want to honour.'

'A good idea, Haman,' approved Xerxes. 'Hurry and dress Mordecai in my royal robes and lead him through the city.' So the furious Haman had to honour Mordecai instead of having him put to death.

### The enemy is discovered

That evening the king and Haman had dinner with Esther again, and the king asked Esther once more what he could do to make her happy.

'Please save me and my people because we're all about to be killed,' Esther said.

'Who would dare to kill you, Queen Esther?' demanded Xerxes.

'Haman is the enemy of my people,' Esther replied, and for the first time she told the king that she was Jewish.

'And Haman has actually built a high gallows on which to hang Mordecai, the Jew who saved your Majesty's life!' one of the attendants added.

'Hang Haman on his own gallows,' ordered the king. So Haman was led out and executed, and then Esther told the king that Mordecai was her cousin.

'He can come to my palace and be second in the empire to me,' declared the king.

As soon as Mordecai came to the palace, he and Esther begged Xerxes to save the Jews who were still in danger from the law Haman had persuaded the king to pass. 'I can't change my proclamation, but I can allow your people to defend themselves,' said the king.

So throughout the empire the Jews were allowed to fight the men who came to execute them. Instead of being killed themselves they managed to put their enemies to death. The next day they celebrated their victory with parties and feasts. They gave presents to one another and made sure that the poor people who couldn't afford presents or even enough food, received special gifts. Mordecai sent letters throughout the kingdom telling everyone to make this celebration every year. To this very day Jewish people keep this special holiday called Purim.

They give one another presents and in some places there is dancing in the streets as they remember how God used the bravery of Esther, the orphan girl who became queen of the Persian Empire, to save the Jewish people from destruction all those years ago.

# GOD'S BUILDERS

### *Back to Jerusalem*

After Nebuchadnezzar took all his prisoners away from Jerusalem the city lay in ruins for many years. The people who were left were too poor to start rebuilding, and they had no leaders to encourage them. In spite of this, the Jewish people who had been taken to Babylon never lost hope that one day Jerusalem would be a proper city again, and they would be able to go home.

'God promised that he would take us back to rebuild Jerusalem,' the old people encouraged their grandchildren. 'One day we will go back.'

At last a king of Babylon called Cyrus decided that the people of his empire should be allowed to live in freedom. He wrote a royal command, and sent it out through all the lands he ruled.

'I am Cyrus, great and mighty, monarch of the whole world,' it said. 'I honour God, and I want people to worship in freedom and peace throughout my lands. Now the Jews live far from their homeland and their Temple is in ruins. I give this command to everyone. You must help the Jews who are to return home and rebuild their Temple. Give them whatever they need, whether it's donkeys to carry their loads, or silver, or gold, or food for the journey, or gifts to put in the Temple.'

Cyrus himself gave them back the treasures which had been stolen from their Temple years before by Nebuchadnezzar: jugs, cups and bowls of gold and silver. Then a party of the Jewish exiles set off for the homeland most of them had never seen. It was over fifty years since their families had first been taken from Jerusalem.

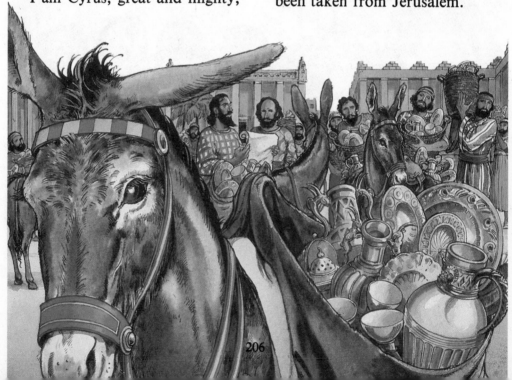

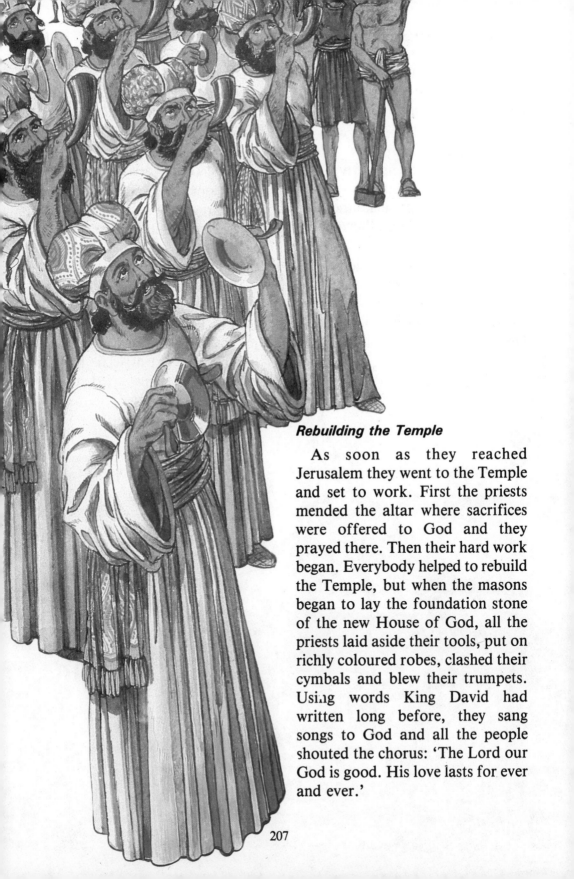

### Rebuilding the Temple

As soon as they reached Jerusalem they went to the Temple and set to work. First the priests mended the altar where sacrifices were offered to God and they prayed there. Then their hard work began. Everybody helped to rebuild the Temple, but when the masons began to lay the foundation stone of the new House of God, all the priests laid aside their tools, put on richly coloured robes, clashed their cymbals and blew their trumpets. Using words King David had written long before, they sang songs to God and all the people shouted the chorus: 'The Lord our God is good. His love lasts for ever and ever.'

Some of the people who lived in the country round Jerusalem asked if they could help to rebuild the Temple, too, but the Jews wouldn't let them.

'You worship idols as well as God. You'll stop us from worshipping God properly, and besides we know you don't really want us to come back and live here,' they said. The other people were furious.

'Who do these newcomers from Babylon think they are?' they asked. They did all they could to frighten the Jewish exiles away. They even bribed the king's officials to spread bad stories about the Jews. When King Cyrus died these men went on telling stories to the new king.

So the Jewish people, who had returned with such high hopes to their homeland, lost heart and stopped their work.

But not for long. Two men still believed God's promises that Jerusalem and its Temple would be rebuilt and would belong to God once more.

'We can't stop now,' they said. 'We must keep on rebuilding in God's name.' Two more men joined them and bravely began to build again, but officials from the new king Darius tried to stop them.

'King Cyrus himself ordered us to rebuild the Temple,' the four friends replied boldly. This was reported back to King Darius who ordered all the scrolls in the royal palace to be searched for King Cyrus's decree. At last it was found, and then Darius issued his own order. 'The work must go on without any more interference, just as Cyrus wanted. Anyone who disobeys my order, or tries to destroy this new Temple will be put to death!' Now the building went ahead smoothly and soon the new Temple was ready. From all over

palace to be searched for King Cyrus's decree. At last it was found, and then Darius issued his own order. 'The work must go on without any more interference, just as Cyrus wanted. Anyone who the country Jewish people who loved God came to Jerusalem and met in the new Temple to pray.

'We've seen how God has made the kings of Babylon agree to let us rebuild the Temple,' they said.

Many years passed. Although the Temple had been rebuilt, many Jewish people still lived in Babylon. Among them was a man called Ezra who was a priest. He loved God and spent his time studying the holy laws so that he would know how to please God and how to teach others to do the same.

At last Ezra decided to go back to Jerusalem to teach the people there more about God. The king gave him permission to go and loaded him with treasure for the Temple. Other people joined Ezra and they went back to Jerusalem together.

When they arrived Ezra took the treasure which the king of Babylon had given him, to the Temple. The priests checked it all carefully and wrote down what was there. Now the Temple was richly furnished again, but Jerusalem itself was a sad, ruined city with many enemies. Its gateways were broken and its walls still lay in ruins.

keep on threatening us and the city is still in ruins.'

Nehemiah went away and prayed for a long time. 'Please rescue your people, Lord,' Nehemiah prayed. 'Use me to help them. May the king listen to my requests for help for Jerusalem.'

Then he got ready and went and poured out the king's wine.

'You look so sad, today, Nehemiah,' the king observed. 'I know you're not ill, so what else is the matter?'

Nehemiah was afraid. The king's servants were not supposed to look sad in front of him, but he answered boldly, 'I'm feeling sad because Jerusalem is still in ruins.'

'Is there anything I can do to help?' asked the king, for Nehemiah's words touched his heart.

Nehemiah said a quick silent prayer to God and then he made his important request to the king.

'Your Majesty, let me go back to Jerusalem to rebuild the city.'

'Of course you can go,' agreed the king at once. 'I can see how much all this means to you. Can I do anything else for you?'

'Sir, I'll need letters signed by you to allow me safe travel through your lands and when I get to Jerusalem I'll need timber for the rebuilding.'

'You shall have everything you need,' promised the king.

**Nehemiah asks the king for help**

Among the Jewish exiles who still lived at the king's court in the city of Susa was a man called Nehemiah. He poured out the king's wine and always tasted it first in case it had been poisoned. The king trusted Nehemiah completely.

One day Nehemiah's brother arrived from Jerusalem. 'Things are very bad indeed,' he told Nehemiah sadly. 'Our enemies

### Repairing the city walls

Nehemiah travelled safely to Jerusalem, but at first he didn't tell anyone why he had come.

That night he got on his donkey and rode all round the city walls. No one saw him set out. He examined the ruined walls carefully. In some places the walls were flattened so badly that heaps of stones lay across Nehemiah's path. The donkey couldn't clamber over them, but Nehemiah guided him round them and came back to the walls again. When he had inspected everything thoroughly he went back home.

Next morning he met some of the priests and leading people of the town and told them his plans.

'God will help us to rebuild the walls,' he encouraged them. 'He's helped me already. I travelled from Susa in complete safety and I've even ᵪot letters from the king giving us permission to repair the walls.'

'What a good idea!' they agreed and the work went ahead at once.

Everyone in Jerusalem wanted to help. Nehemiah divided them all into groups and put each group in charge of a different section of the wall so that no one had too much to do.

But the Jews still had enemies in the land round Jerusalem. Among them was a man called Sanballat, the foreign governor of Samaria, who did not want the Jews to have their own strong city and grow powerful again. At first he and his friends laughed at Nehemiah. 'What do those Jews think they're doing? Why it only needs a fox to jump on the walls and they'd fall down!' Soon, however, their sneers turned to threats, and

Nehemiah decided he would have to guard the wall with sentries. He divided the workmen into two parties. Half worked on building while the other half kept watch. Even those who were working carried weapons, but the people were still frightened.

'Remember that God is with us,' Nehemiah reminded them. 'He's far stronger than our enemies. He won't let us be defeated now.'

Just the same, so that they would feel less alarmed, Nehemiah had a bugler standing beside him ready to sound an alarm and warn the builders scattered all along the walls in case the enemy attacked.

Everyone worked from the first light of dawn until the stars appeared in the sky, and Nehemiah and his men did sentry work all night as well. In the seven weeks it took to rebuild the walls Nehemiah didn't get undressed to go to bed. He simply snatched a few hours' sleep and then worked on.

As well as building the walls, Nehemiah had the job of governor of Judah, the whole country round Jerusalem. He knew that the people were poor and had to pay heavy taxes so he never took any money from them himself, even though he was allowed to do so. Instead he provided food for many of the Jews and their leaders, and paid for it himself. Every day one hundred and fifty people sat round his tables, eating a whole ox, six sheep and a large number of chickens as well as drinking jars of wine.

Not everyone was so generous and some of the poor people brought their complaints to Nehemiah. 'We're so poor we even have to borrow money to buy bread, and when we can't pay it back the rich people take our land and goods. They even make our children slaves,' they said. Nehemiah was so furious that he called all the rich people together at once.

'Don't you know that in Babylon we actually collect money to buy back Jews who are sold as slaves?' he said. 'Yet here in Jerusalem you force your fellow

citizens to make their own children your slaves. Why, God tells us in his law how wrong that is, and well you know it! Now give back

214

everything you've taken from the poor people, especially their children!'

The rich leaders agreed, and that day many poor families in Jerusalem were made very happy because of what Nehemiah had done.

Nehemiah's enemies kept trying to trick him into leaving Jerusalem to meet them, so that they could seize him and kill him. 'My work's far too important to stop just so that I can meet you,' Nehemiah replied. But within himself he prayed, 'Please, Lord, help me to be stronger than my enemies.'

One day a man called Shemaiah who claimed to be a prophet asked him to his house. 'Oh, Nehemiah, I'm glad you've come,' the man greeted him, when he arrived. 'God has given me a message for you. You've to hide in the Temple because your enemies could arrive any minute now and kill you.'

'Do you think I would run away and hide to save my own skin?' Nehemiah demanded in surprise. He left the man's house at once, but later he realised that Sanballat had bribed Shemaiah to persuade him to run away. Then they could tell everyone what a coward Nehemiah was and disgrace him.

Yet in spite of all the trouble the walls were built.

'Now everyone knows that God is with us. We could never have done this without his help,' Nehemiah declared.

## Ezra reads God's laws to the people

When all the work was over, everyone gathered together to worship God.

'Let's ask Ezra, the priest, to explain God's laws to us,' they said. A wooden platform was hastily set up in the city square so

that everyone would be able to see Ezra clearly and hear what he said. Families crowded round to listen. Ezra unrolled the heavy scroll on which the law was written and stood up.

'Let's thank God together,' said Ezra. At once the whole crowd lifted their hands high in the air and praised God. Ezra explained the law carefully. He reminded them of all that God had done for them, and the way they had to behave to please him, by not worshipping idols or adopting the ways of other nations. Everyone listened and soon they began to cry.

'We haven't kept God's law properly,' they said, in tears.

'But God wants us to worship him joyfully,' Nehemiah comforted them. 'So cheer up and let's enjoy our party because we're trying to make today a special one for God.'

So everyone cheered up and shared their food with one another. No one went hungry that day.

### Festival time

They all wanted to keep the old festivals that had meant so much to their people in the past, and which were described in detail in the law that Ezra had read to them.

'It's time to keep the Festival of Shelters,' Ezra announced. 'Long ago when our people wandered through the desert to the country God promised to give them, they had no houses to live in but they trusted in God and he looked after them. We're learning to trust God, too, and so we'll keep the festival properly and camp out for a week in little huts as the law tells us.'

Everyone followed Ezra's instructions with great excitement. First they went out into the country and gathered branches of olive, pine, myrtle and palm which they wove into little huts. They camped out in the huts for a week and read from God's law every day. In the evenings they danced and sang together.

Although everyone enjoyed these festivals, perhaps the best celebration of all was the one they had when the walls were finally finished. Singers and musicians came to lead everyone in 'thank-you' songs. Nehemiah divided the people into two groups. Ezra led one group along the top of the new walls in one direction, while Nehemiah led the second group the other way. Trumpeters marched on ahead and everyone followed, singing at the top of their voices until they all met at the Temple.

There they offered sacrifices and the singing went on and on. The music of trumpets, harps and cymbals sounded across the newly-built walls. People danced and clapped. The noise they made could be heard from far and wide. 'God has answered all our prayers,' said Nehemiah to Ezra. 'Jerusalem is rebuilt and the law is obeyed by our people again.'

### God promises a special king

The people went on worshipping God and caring about what he wanted. They wrote down the stories of the Jewish people and the way God had looked after them. They remembered Abraham, Isaac, Jacob and Joseph and how God had been their friend. They thought about how Moses had rescued the people of Israel from Egypt and led them safely across the Red Sea and taught them God's law. They sang the 'thank-you' songs which King David had written, and they learnt King Solomon's wise sayings. They began to understand the message that Jeremiah and the other prophets had tried to teach – that God wanted them to love him and be his friends.

Above all they learnt that God was going to send them a new special king, someone who would be even greater than King David.

'He will come to us as a small child, and he will be called the Prince of Peace,' they said. 'His kingdom will last until the end of time. He will always obey God and do what pleases him. He won't let anyone cheat, and he won't hurt the weak. He will even take the punishment we deserve from God on himself, although he has done nothing to deserve it.'

Eagerly the people waited for the promised king to be born.

# OLD TESTAMENT

| DATE BC | PEOPLE AND EVENTS |
|---------|-------------------|
| 2000 | |
| | *Abraham leaves Ur of the Chaldees for Canaan* |
| 1900 | |
| | *Isaac* |
| 1800 | |
| | *Jacob and Esau* |
| | *Joseph is taken to Egypt as a slave* |
| 1700 | |
| | *Jacob's family settle in Egypt* |
| 1600 | |
| 1500 | |
| | *Hebrews become slaves in Egypt* |
| 1400 | |
| | *Moses adopted by Pharaoh's daughter* |
| 1300 | |
| | *Moses leads the Hebrews out of Egypt* |
| | *Hebrews cross Jordan and enter Canaan* |
| | *Fall of Jericho* |
| 1200 | |
| | *Ruth and Naomi settle in Bethlehem* |
| | *Gideon defeats the Midianites* |
| 1100 | |
| | *Samson attacks the Philistines* |
| | *The boy Samuel goes to live in the Temple* |
| | *Saul becomes first King of Israel* |
| 1000 | |
| | *David kills Goliath* |
| | *Solomon builds the Temple in Jerusalem* |
| | *The Kingdom is divided into Israel and Judah* |
| 900 | |
| | *Elijah challenges the Prophets of Baal* |
| | *Elisha travels teaching about God* |
| 800 | |
| 700 | |
| | *Jeremiah urges the people to worship God* |
| | *Babylonians invade Judah* |
| 600 | |
| | *Daniel in the lions' den* |
| | *Temple in Jerusalem rebuilt* |
| 500 | |
| | *Esther, Queen of Persia, saves the Jews* |
| | *Nehemiah and the rebuilding of Jerusalem* |
| 400 | |

# NEW TESTAMENT

| DATE | PEOPLE AND EVENTS | | |
|------|-------------------|---|---|
| | | | Palestine ruled by Herod the Great |
| 10 BC | | | |
| 0 | | Birth of Jesus | |
| 10 AD | | | |
| 20 | | | |
| | | Baptism of Jesus Jesus' death and Resurrection | Pontius Pilate Roman Procurator |
| 30 | | | |
| | Paul's conversion | | |
| 40 | | | |
| | Paul's 1st Missionary Journey Paul's 2nd Missionary Journey | | |
| 50 | | | |
| | Paul's 3rd Missionary Journey Paul imprisoned in Caesarea | | |
| 60 | | | |
| | Paul taken to Rome Christians persecuted by Emperor Nero Fall of Jerusalem to Romans | | |
| 70 | | | |
| 80 | | | |
| | Christians persecuted by Emperor Domitian | | |
| 90 | | | |
| | Death of Apostle John | | |
| 100 | | | |

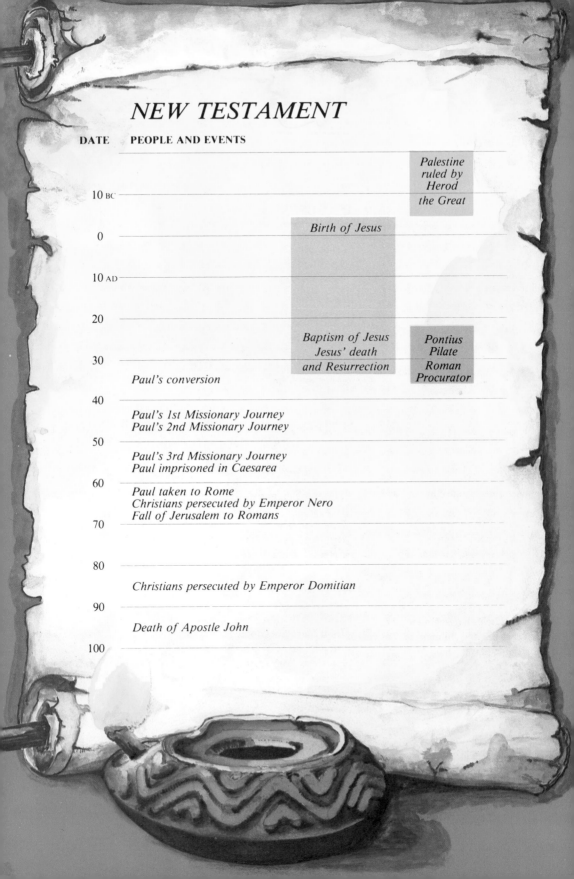

# New Testament Contents

## Jesus the Child

Mary and the angel 226
Mary and Joseph 226
The journey to Bethlehem 227
In the stable 229
The shepherds' king 230
The wise men 232
Escape to Egypt 234
The boy Jesus 235

## Jesus Begins His Special Work

John the Baptist 237
Jesus in the desert 238
Jesus goes to a wedding 240
Jesus calls the fishermen 241
Jesus makes the sick well 242
Jesus and a lame man 243
Jesus and a tax-collector 244
Jesus and Nicodemus 245
Jesus and a Samaritan woman 246
Jesus and his Father 248

## Jesus the Storyteller

The good shepherd 250
The missing sheep 251
The flowers 253
The wonderful harvest 254
The two houses 256
The two men 257
The lost son 258
The good Samaritan 262

## Jesus the Friend

Keeping the Sabbath 266
Jesus helps a Roman soldier 268
Jesus calms a storm 269
Jesus feeds five thousand people 270
Jesus helps ten sick men 272
Jesus and the children 273
Jesus and the rich young man 274
Jesus and the little tax-collector 274
Jesus and the blind beggar 276
Jesus and the two sisters 278
Jesus raises Lazarus 279

## The Easter Story

Jesus goes to Jerusalem 282
Jesus clears the temple 284
Jesus and the poor widow 286
Jesus and the expensive perfume 286
Jesus and Judas 288
The Passover meal 288
Judas betrays Jesus 290
Jesus is arrested 292
Peter lets Jesus down 294
Jesus and the Roman governor 295
Jesus is crucified 296
Jesus is alive 299
A walk to Emmaus 302
Jesus meets his friends 304
Jesus and Thomas 305
Jesus and Peter 306
Jesus goes back to Heaven 307

## The First Christians

The new helper 309
Peter and John heal a lame man 311
Peter and John in trouble 312
More trouble 314
Stephen 316
Philip in Samaria 319
The Ethiopian treasurer 320
Saul meets Jesus 322
Saul escapes from Damascus 325
The churches grow 327
Dorcas 327
Peter's dream 328
Peter and Cornelius 329
Peter in prison 330

## Paul the Traveller

Saul goes to Antioch 332
Saul and Elymas 334
John Mark goes home 335
Jupiter and Mercury 336
Paul and Barnabas disagree 337
Two new helpers 339
The friends go to Greece 340
Paul and Silas in prison 340
The jailer 341
Trouble in Thessalonica 343
Paul in Athens 345
Priscilla and Aquila 346
Paul's third journey 348
Riot in Ephesus 349
Eutychus 351
Paul says goodbye to the Ephesians 352
Agabus' message 353

## Paul the Prisoner

Paul in danger 354
Paul is arrested 355
Paul before the council 356
The plot 357
Paul goes before Felix 361
The new governor 361
Paul sets sail 363
Paul and the snake 366
The governor's father 366

## Paul's Letters

Onesimus 368
Parents and children 369
The great race 370
A letter to Timothy 371

## The Work Goes On

The Christians in Rome 372

## John's Vision

John sees Jesus 373
Letters to the churches 374
God as King 375
The new Jerusalem 376

# THE NEW TESTAMENT

# JESUS THE CHILD

### Mary and the angel

This is the story of Jesus and the first of his followers. It began nearly two thousand years ago in Nazareth, a little village in the land of Israel. A young woman named Mary was getting the dinner ready. Beans and yellow peas bubbled in the pot on the stove, and Mary was mixing dough for the barley bread. It seemed just like any other evening.

Suddenly a voice called her name. She looked up amazed; a stranger stood beside her. Light shone from his face, even his clothes seemed full of light. He was an angel sent from God.

'The Lord is with you, Mary,' the angel said. 'He is pleased with you. He will make a baby grow inside you; a little boy whose name is to be Jesus. He is God's own Son, the promised king who will save his people from the wrongdoing and wickedness that keep them from knowing God.'

At first Mary did not understand the angel, then she said, 'I am the Lord's servant. I will do whatever he wants.'

### Mary and Joseph

Mary was going to be married to a man called Joseph who was the village carpenter. When he heard about the baby, Joseph thought he should not marry Mary after all. Then an angel spoke to him in a dream and told him that God had sent the baby to Mary. The angel

told Joseph to marry her, and Joseph believed the angel and did as he said.

### The journey to Bethlehem

One day, soon after their wedding, Joseph said to Mary, 'I have some news for you, dear. Our rulers, the Romans, have ordered everyone to go back to the towns where they were born, to have their

names put on a register. They are trying to count everyone in our country so that they can tax them. My family comes from Bethlehem so we must go there. I'm afraid it will be a hard journey for you,' added Joseph, anxiously.

'God will look after us,' said Mary quietly. She knew that the Romans could not be disobeyed. Their soldiers had conquered Israel, and their Emperor ruled the land.

So they set off. Soon they joined other travellers, all making their way across the rocky countryside to Bethlehem. At night they camped by the roadside, sleeping on the ground with only a fire to keep the wild beasts away. Then, at last, Joseph pointed to a little walled town on a hillside ahead.

'There we are, nearly there now!' he said.

'I shall be glad to get to an inn,' said Mary. 'I can feel that my baby will be born soon!'

'Then we must hurry! Bethlehem is the town where King David was born, hundreds of years ago. Our teachers have often told us that another special leader will

be born in Bethlehem. He is the one who will guide our people in God's ways.'

'Hurry, little donkey!' said Mary. 'The teachers were right. Our baby king, Jesus, will be born tonight in Bethlehem. God is watching over us!'

### In the stable

The streets of Bethlehem were crowded with tired travellers.

'I have no room anywhere. We're packed out!' cried the innkeeper.

'Please,' Mary begged, 'my baby will be born very soon. Can't you help at all?'

'I wish I could, dear!' the innkeeper answered. 'Wait a minute, though . . . you can sleep in the stable! The straw's clean enough, and the cows will keep you warm. Look – this way . . .'

The stable was little more than a cave, but later that night, Jesus, God's own Son was born there, and Mary laid him in a manger filled with hay, because there was no room for him in the busy inn.

### The shepherds' king

No one in the crowded town knew that the promised king was lying asleep in the stable, but an angel told the news to some shepherds who were looking after their sheep in the fields outside Bethlehem.

'News! Good news for everyone!' The shepherds looked up, terrified. A great company of angels, brighter than the starlit sky, crowded round them.

'Don't be afraid,' said one. 'Your promised king, your Saviour Christ the Lord, has been born close by in Bethlehem. You'll find him there, wrapped in linen cloths,

lying in a manger. Go quickly and see!'

Then the shepherds heard the angels singing, 'Glory to the most high God! Peace to his people on earth!'

They left their sheep and hurried up the hill to Bethlehem.

Trying not to make too much noise, they crowded into the stable and knelt beside the manger where Jesus slept on the hay.

When they saw the tiny baby, they whispered joyfully, 'O, praise God! Thank God! He has sent this little one to be our Saviour. The promised king has been born in a stable, not in a rich palace. God has not forgotten us, his poor people!'

The shepherds hurried away, still praising God. Mary sat and watched her baby boy.

'It's dark in the stable. The cows moo and stamp. Rats rustle in the hay, but the music of highest heaven plays for you, dear Jesus. Sleep well, little one, sleep well,' Mary murmured.

## The wise men

Far away in the desert, wise men were riding towards Bethlehem, following a huge star that blazed in the sky. Each dry hot day they rested, shaded by their kneeling camels, but at night they rode on, following the star. The cold wind stung their faces as they gazed at the sky.

'The star tells me that a king is born,' said one. 'I am old, yet when I saw the star I left my home and my books to follow it and find the king.'

'It must be guiding us to a royal palace. Surely that is where we shall find such an important baby!' said another.

So when they came to the city of Jerusalem, where the royal palace of Israel was, they went no further, but stopped to look for the baby.

The king who lived there was called Herod. He welcomed the wise men, but their news alarmed him.

'A star tells these visitors that a new king has been born in my kingdom!' he thought angrily. 'There's only room for one king in this country, and that's me!'

He turned to the priests who stood near him. 'Where is the promised king to be born?' he asked.

'In Bethlehem, O King!' they answered, bowing low.

'I must get rid of this baby!' thought Herod, and he made a cunning plan.

'Search for the child in Bethlehem,' he told the wise men. 'When you find him, let me know. I want to worship him, too.'

Herod was lying. Really he wanted to kill the baby.

The wise men found Mary and Joseph and the baby in Bethlehem. They knelt and worshipped Jesus. They had brought gifts for him – bright gold, sweet-smelling myrrh and frankincense.

Then God warned the wise men not to trust King Herod. So they did not tell him where Jesus was, but made their way home without going back to Jerusalem.

### Escape to Egypt

That night an angel came to Joseph in a dream.

'Herod is looking for the baby to kill him,' said the angel. 'Get up quickly, take baby Jesus and Mary and go to Egypt. Stay there until I tell you to leave.'

So Joseph woke Mary and the baby, and the family escaped from the town.

'I heard the sound of children crying when we crept out of Bethlehem,' said Mary as she followed Joseph along the road.

'I heard it, too,' said Joseph. 'Herod's soldiers are killing all the baby boys in the town. He wanted to kill our baby king. That's why God has told us to escape to the land of Egypt.'

So the little family lived in Egypt until King Herod died and it was safe for them to go back home to Nazareth.

## The boy Jesus

In Nazareth the boy Jesus grew up, sturdy and strong. He used to help Joseph in the carpenter's shop. No one in the village knew about the angels who had sung when he was born in Bethlehem, or about the star and the wise men with their costly gifts. Only Mary would sometimes watch her son and wonder what would happen to him.

Then, when Jesus was twelve, he went with his parents to Jerusalem for the great Passover festival. It was wonderful to climb the steep narrow streets to the golden temple! Long after the other families from Nazareth had gone home, Jesus stayed on. He spoke to the wise teachers who taught the people about God.

'Who is this boy?' the learned men wondered. 'He seems to know God in such a special way. He is completely at home here in God's house.'

Meanwhile Joseph and Mary were travelling back to Nazareth. They supposed that Jesus was with them, somewhere in the party of friends and relations. They had made a whole day's journey before they noticed that Jesus was missing. They went all the way back to Jerusalem, looking for him.

At last they found him in the temple.

'Why have you done this to us?' Mary asked. 'We've been so worried about you, we've been looking for you everywhere!'

'Didn't you expect to find me here, in my Father's house?' Jesus answered, but he went quietly home with his parents.

Mary did not understand what he meant then, but she often thought about his words. When Jesus grew up and started to do the special work that God, his Father, had planned for him, she remembered and understood.

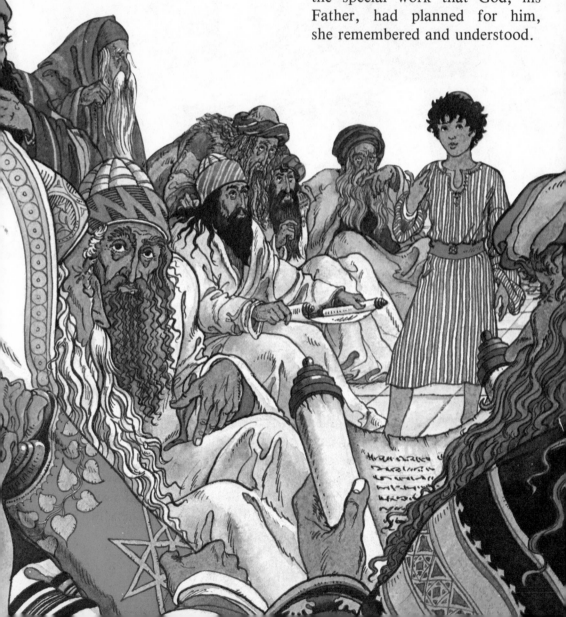

# JESUS BEGINS HIS SPECIAL WORK

## *John the Baptist*

So the years passed by until at last it was nearly time for Jesus to put away his carpenter's tools and go to do the special work which God had planned for him.

At about this time Jesus' cousin John left his home and went to live in the desert beyond the River Jordan. He wore rough clothes made from camel hair and ate the food of the desert: locusts — creatures like large grasshoppers — and wild honey.

Every day John would stand by the banks of the river and teach the people about God. His eyes glowed like the hot sun and his voice, strong as the desert wind, drew large crowds who flocked to hear John's news about the king that God was going to send.

'You are all doing wrong things, things that make God angry,' John cried. 'You must stop, and start to lead good lives so that God can forgive you. I will baptise you here in the Jordan as a sign that you are sorry. There isn't much time! We know that God promised to give us a special king to lead us. He will come soon, and we must be ready for him!'

237

One day Jesus came to the river and asked John to baptise him, too. John knew at once that Jesus was God's promised king. At first he did not want to baptise Jesus, but Jesus knew that this was what God wanted, even though he had done nothing wrong. So humbly, John baptised him.

As they came up from the water they heard the voice of God himself saying, 'This is my own dear Son. I am very pleased with him.'

## Jesus in the desert

Then Jesus left the crowds on the river bank and went by himself into the desert. There was nowhere for him to shelter from the scorching midday sun or the cold wind that blew at night. Wild animals roamed across the sands and evil lurked there.

When Jesus had been alone for forty days the Devil came to test him. He wanted Jesus to use the power he had as God's Son to win

praise for himself instead of carrying out God's work. The Devil knew that Jesus had no food to eat, so first of all he tried to persuade him to turn the desert stones into bread. Jesus refused.

'People need more than bread to stay alive,' he told the Devil. 'They need to know the words of God, and to obey them, too.'

The Devil tried again. He took Jesus to the highest tower of the temple in Jerusalem.

'Jump down!' he said. 'Don't be afraid! You won't hurt yourself. The holy writings teach that God will send his angels to catch you!'

'The holy writings also say that we must not try to test God!' Jesus replied.

Then the Devil showed Jesus the kingdoms of the world with all their power and wealth.

'I will give all this to you if you will just kneel down and worship me!' the Devil said.

'Go away, Devil!' Jesus answered, sternly. 'God is the only one we should worship.'

Defeated, the Devil left him alone, and God sent angels to strengthen him after his test.

Now Jesus was ready to go back to the people who lived in the towns and villages round about and teach them about God.

## Jesus goes to a wedding

One day Jesus and some of his friends were invited to a wedding with Mary, Jesus' mother. Everyone enjoyed the party afterwards, but after a while Mary's friend came over to her.

'What shall we do?' she asked. 'We've run out of wine!'

It was a disgrace not to be able to offer wine to the guests all through the wedding party. Mary felt sorry for her friend. She told Jesus what had happened. Then she spoke to the servants. 'My son Jesus will help. Just do whatever he tells you!'

There were six huge jars standing near the door. Jesus told the servants to fill them with water.

'Now take some out and give it to the best man,' he said, when the jars were full.

One of the servants filled a jug. He waited anxiously while the best man drank. Would he be angry at being offered water? But the best man smiled.

'This is the best wine I have ever tasted; fancy saving it until last!' he exclaimed.

Jesus had turned all the water into wine! Now everyone could enjoy the celebrations.

### Jesus calls the fishermen

Not far from the town where the wedding was held lay a large lake called the Sea of Galilee. One afternoon two fishermen sat mending their nets on the shore where the fishing boats were beached. Their names were Peter and Andrew.

Two children came by and stopped to watch.

'Jesus is coming this way,' the children said. 'We saw him back there along the shore.'

Simon and Andrew looked up quickly. Simon had met Jesus before, and he wanted to talk to him again.

Then they saw Jesus in the distance, calling them.

'Simon! Andrew! Leave your nets! Come with me! I want you to help me to tell everyone about God!'

At once the fishermen leapt to their feet. They waved goodbye to the children and set off after Jesus.

Further up the beach two more fishermen, called James and John, were working in their boat with their father. They were cousins of Jesus, like John who had baptised him.

'Come with us,' Jesus called to them. 'I need your help, too.' So the two men said goodbye to their father and went with Jesus.

### Jesus makes the sick well

Simon, who was also known as Peter, invited them all to come home with him.

'My wife and her mother will be so pleased to see you, Jesus!' he said.

Simon Peter did not know that his wife's mother was ill. They found her in bed.

'Oh, dear Teacher,' she said when she saw Jesus, 'I would like to have given you a proper welcome, but then I felt so hot and weak I had to lie down . . .'

Jesus bent down and touched the old woman's hand. She felt better immediately. In fact, she got up at once and cooked them a delicious meal.

That evening crowds of sick people gathered outside Simon's house. Those who couldn't walk were carried by their friends. Children led their elderly, ailing grandparents, mothers brought their sick babies, and blind people were guided there. People who were possessed by evil spirits, and sad people, whose worries made them ill, came too. Jesus helped them all. He touched the sick and made them well. He drove away the evil spirits. Everyone discovered that God cared about them and had sent Jesus to help them, and make them well again.

### Jesus and a lame man

More and more people wanted Jesus to heal their sick friends and relatives. One day four men brought a lame friend to the house where Jesus was staying. Their friend had been lame for twenty years. He couldn't walk at all, and his friends had to carry him on a mattress. When they reached the house they couldn't get in because of the crowds round the door. So they went up on to the roof, which was flat and made of mud, and began to scrape a hole large enough to let their friend through. The mud crumbled away easily, and soon they could lower their friend down to Jesus.

Jesus looked at the man and said, 'Everything you've done wrong is forgiven. Now you will be able to get up and walk.'

Some of the Jewish leaders, the priests and scribes who taught the people about God and his laws, were standing in the crowd, watching. They were shocked and angry.

'Only God can forgive people like that,' they said. 'Who does Jesus think he is?'

But the man stood up happily. He thanked Jesus and hurried out, running and jumping on his legs that were strong again.

### Jesus and a tax-collector

Now Jesus chose someone else to help him – Matthew, the tax-collector. The tax-men collected money from the people to give to their Roman rulers. Nobody liked the Romans, who had taken over Palestine, and they despised the tax-collectors who worked for them. To make matters worse, the tax-collectors often cheated the people, taking money for themselves as well.

No one spoke to tax-collectors unless they had to, but Jesus went straight to the table where Matthew was working.

'Follow me!' he said.

At once Matthew decided to leave his money bags and rolls of accounts. He got to his feet and hurried away with Jesus. That evening he held a party so that other tax-collectors could meet Jesus, too. The Jewish leaders and some of the other bystanders were shocked to see Jesus mixing with such dishonest people, but Jesus explained, 'Bad people need me, too. In fact they are the very ones I have come to help.'

### Jesus and Nicodemus

All this puzzled the religious leaders. When Jesus made people well and taught them so wisely it seemed to prove that he came from God. Yet because he mixed with bad people he seemed to be breaking God's holy laws. One of the religious leaders, a man called Nicodemus, was so puzzled that one night after dark, when the city was deserted and there was no one to see, Nicodemus went to find Jesus.

They talked together for a long time. Jesus answered Nicodemus' questions and explained many things to him. At last Nicodemus went home very thoughtfully. He decided to become a follower of Jesus too, but he kept it a secret for a long time.

### Jesus and a Samaritan woman

Jesus and his friends used to go round the countryside together, teaching people about God's ways. One hot day they were travelling through a district called Samaria. The others went off to buy food, while Jesus rested beside a well.

A Samaritan woman came by for some water. She didn't speak to Jesus, for Samaritans and Jews were enemies and never spoke to one another. In any case, a Jewish man would not usually speak to a woman if he met her outside her home. To her surprise, however, Jesus asked her for a drink of water.

'Why are you asking me?' she exclaimed. Soon they were deep in conversation. As Jesus talked, the woman's amazement grew. Jesus knew all about her, even about the wrong things she had done, but he still wanted to help her to learn more about God. Greatly impressed, she decided to bring her friends to meet him. Many of them believed Jesus' message about God, and they asked him to stay with them and teach them more. Jesus was only too pleased to agree and he stayed two more days with the Samaritan woman and her friends.

### Jesus and his Father

One day Jesus took Peter, James and John into the hills. They climbed a high, lonely mountain and Jesus went ahead to pray. As the fishermen watched they saw his face shining. His clothes dazzled them with a whiteness brighter than snow in sunshine. Jesus stood bathed in light. Two

men stood talking to him. They were Moses and Elijah, two long-dead leaders of the Jewish people. Amazed, Peter called out to Jesus. At that moment a shining cloud covered them, and from it came the voice of God himself: 'This is my dear Son. Listen to him!'

The fishermen fell on their faces in fear. When they dared to look up again, Moses and Elijah had gone. Only Jesus stood beside them, telling them not to be afraid. Slowly they went down the mountain. Now they knew that Jesus really was God's Son, but they still did not understand everything that this meant. They only realised later when Jesus had died and come to life again, as he had said he would. Jesus himself told them to say nothing about what they had seen until that happened.

# JESUS THE STORYTELLER

## *The good shepherd*

By now large crowds followed Jesus wherever he went, and he taught them about God. Jesus always spoke simply, and he didn't make things difficult to understand, as their leaders often did. Instead he told them interesting stories. Here are some of the stories that Jesus told.

Once there was a shepherd who looked after his sheep so well he knew exactly which ones belonged to him even when they were in a big sheepfold with lots of other flocks. The shepherd soon sorted out his sheep from the rest. He

knew their names too and he called to each one. The sheep understood because they recognized their shepherd's voice. They followed him as he walked ahead of them, showing them the way to places where the grass was good and it was safe for his flock to graze. Whenever thieves tried to steal the sheep or wolves attacked them the shepherd never ran away like some bad shepherds did. He stayed with his sheep and fought off their attackers, even if he hurt himself

'I am just like the good shepherd,' Jesus explained. 'And the people who follow me are like those sheep – I look after them. I shall even give my life for them.'

### The missing sheep

The second story was about a shepherd who had a hundred sheep to look after.

One evening when he counted them he found there were only ninety nine. A sheep was missing! What had happened to it? Had it been stolen? Had it wandered away and been eaten by a lion, or fallen over a cliff? The shepherd was very sad and very worried. He left the ninety nine sheep in the pasture and went into the hills to search for the missing one.

At last he found it, high on a crag in the mountains. The shepherd was delighted. He heaved the frightened animal on to his strong shoulders and carried it safely back to the flock. Then he called his friends together: 'Come on, everyone, I want to celebrate – I'm so happy that my lost sheep is safely back in the fold!'

This story had an extra, secret meaning, too. People who turn their backs on God and forget him are like the sheep which went missing. God is like the shepherd who searched for his one lost sheep and was glad when he found it, even though he still had ninety nine good sheep at home.

## The flowers

Jesus wanted everyone to understand that God cares for people very much and is always ready to help those who trust him. Jesus knew his friends were often worried because they didn't have much money and they had left their jobs to follow him.

'Don't be anxious,' Jesus told them, pointing to the flowers which carpeted the grass by the sea of Galilee. 'Did you ever see a flower sit down to spin its beautiful clothes? Of course not! Yet see how brightly God dresses them! Even rich King Solomon in all his glorious robes never wore anything so splendid! If God takes so much trouble with the grass, won't he take even more care of you and give you clothes and food, too? So why don't you trust him? Expect God to look after you and stop worrying all the time!'

253

## The wonderful harvest

Jesus' stories were always about familiar things like the flowers which everyone had seen. Everyone had seen shepherds working in the hills, too, and they all knew about farmers like the one in this next story.

Early one morning a farmer set out to sow his seed. He carried it in a big bag, and as he walked he scattered handfuls of seed over the ground. Some fell on the hard earth of the path and birds flew down at once and pecked it up. Some seed fell into stony ground where there was only a thin layer of soil. Green shoots sprang up very quickly, but they could not take root in the shallow earth — so as soon as the sun grew hot the young plants dried up and died.

Some of the seed fell among thorn bushes which choked the shoots so that they could not grow.

Some seed, however, fell into good soil where it grew and ripened until it stood thick and tall, ready for the harvest. The farmer was pleased, for the good ground gave back thirty, sixty, even a hundred times more corn than he had sown! It was a wonderful harvest!

After he had told the story, Jesus explained the secret meaning to his friends.

'The seed is our message about God's love. The hard earth path is like the hearts of some people who never accept what we tell them. The message soon disappears from their minds.

'Other people do understand and are thrilled by the message, but they don't want to do anything too hard. When trouble comes they give up easily and blame God. They are like the stony soil which only had a thin layer of good earth.

'Other people listen to our message, but all sorts of worries about money and the problems of everyday life spring up in their minds, like the thorns in the story, and choke the good news about God.

'But there *are* people who are so glad to hear about God's love that they start to lead lives that please him and they tell the good news to others, too. They are like the good soil that gives back more grain than the farmer sowed.'

### The two houses

Jesus told another story about people who listened to his teaching.

'If you follow my teaching,' he said, 'you are like the wise man who wanted to build a house. He dug down through the sandy soil of the valley where he wanted to build it until he came to the rock. Then he built his house firmly, using the rock for a foundation. When the autumn rains came and flooded the valley, and storms shook the house it stood firmly.

'Another man built a house nearby, but he didn't bother to dig down to the rock, instead he built his house on the sand. When the autumn rains came the sandy soil was washed away. The house creaked and shook and came crashing down. The flood swept it away and there was nothing left of it.

'Those who don't follow my teaching are like that. When troubles come they can't stand firm.'

### The two men

Jesus had another story about two very different men who went to pray in the temple. The first was a Pharisee, one of the Jewish leaders, and the second was a tax-collector.

The Pharisee thought he always kept God's laws. He swept proudly in through the temple doors and stood where everyone could see him. Loudly he told God how good he was: 'Thank you God, that I'm better than other people. I'm not a bit like that tax-man over there. I do everything that pleases you.'

The tax-man who had come in very quietly could only whisper with his head bent low, 'Have pity on me, God. I've done wrong and I'm sorry.'

Both men went home, but it was not the proud Pharisee who pleased God most. It was the tax-man who said, 'sorry'; and God forgave him.

parties because he was rich. Before long his money was spent, and his new friends disappeared, too. No one wanted him without money.

### The lost son

In another story, Jesus taught how God is always longing to forgive anyone who owns up like the tax-man did.

A farmer had two sons. The elder was a stay-at-home, but the younger boy loved adventure.

'I want to see the world,' thought the younger son. 'When my father is dead, I'll get a share of his goods, but I want some money now. I'll go and ask my father for my share of his things. Then I'll leave home and do whatever I want.'

The farmer felt very sad that his son wanted to leave home because he loved the boy, but he let him do what he wanted. So, with a purse full of money, the younger son set off for a distant country.

At first he had plenty of fun and made a great many friends who were glad to invite him to their

He was all alone, and he didn't even have enough to buy food. He tried to find work, but the only job he could get was on a farm, looking after pigs.

He watched the pigs guzzling their food and he wished he could have something to eat, too. He would even have been glad to eat some of the pigs' bean pods. He began to think of his home where no one was ever hungry.

'My father is kind and treats everyone well, even the servants,' he thought. 'How stupid I am, sitting here starving! I'll go back home and tell my father I'm sorry. Perhaps he'll let me work for him as a servant if he doesn't want me back as a son!'

The more he thought about it, the better the idea seemed. Feeling happier than he had done for a very long time, the young man set off on his journey home.

Some time later, his father was looking out of the window, when he spotted a thin figure limping

along. The farmer stared. Then he saw that it was his younger son, and he raced down the road to meet him. He flung his arms round him and hugged and kissed him while the boy started to say, 'sorry'.

'Father, I've done wrong in God's eyes, and I've treated you badly, too,' he said. 'I'm not fit to be your son any more, but please take me back to be one of your hired servants.'

His father wouldn't hear of it. He hurried him into the house, calling to his servants, 'Bring the best robe and put it on my son! Give him a ring to wear and sandals, too. Kill the young calf! We'll have a splendid feast!'

The elder son was working for his father in the fields. When he came back to the house in the evening he heard the sound of music and dancing. The servants told him that his brother had come home. He stood in the doorway, sulking.

'Father never killed a calf for me to have a party,' he muttered,

'and I've stayed at the farm working while my brother was away enjoying himself. It's not fair!'

His father had to come out to persuade him to go in to the feast.

'You've always been with me,' he said, 'and everything I have now is yours. But it's right that we should be glad and celebrate today! I thought your brother was dead, but he's come to life again — he was lost, but now he's found!'

## The good Samaritan

As well as teaching people about God and how to please him, Jesus wanted to show people how they should treat one another. Once one of the religious leaders asked Jesus a question. 'What must I do to go to heaven when I die?'

Jesus knew that the questioner was a clever man who was really trying to catch him out, so he asked another question in return.

'God gave us a law to tell us how to please him. What does it say?'

'We must love God with all our heart and love our neighbours just as much as we love ourselves,' answered the man.

'Then that is what you must do,' answered Jesus simply.

'Well, but who is my neighbour?' the clever man asked. And Jesus told a story to answer him.

The road from Jerusalem to Jericho goes through lonely country where there are plenty of rocks for robbers to hide behind. Nobody liked using the road, especially when they were on their own. One day a traveller set out from Jerusalem, and sure enough, before he had gone very far, a gang of thieves leapt out and attacked him. They snatched his bags, stripped off his cloak and beat him up. Then they ran off, leaving him badly hurt. He would certainly die if no one came by to help him.

As he lay there, he heard footsteps coming along the road. He was too weak to shout or move, but he felt sure that whoever it was would see him.

The passerby was a priest. He was going to Jerusalem to pray in the temple. He noticed the man, but he was too scared to stop in case the robbers attacked him, too.

Hastily he crossed over the road and walked by on the other side.

A little later another man came down the road. He was on his way to the temple, too. He looked at the wounded man for a moment, but then he crossed the road as well, and went on his way, leaving the man lying in the hot sun.

At last a Samaritan came by,

riding on a donkey. Jews and
Samaritans hated one another, but
this man felt sorry for the
wounded Jew. He got off his
donkey and searched in his bags
for some cool oil and wine which
he had with him. He used them to
clean the man's cuts. Then he tore
up his own clothes for bandages.
He lifted the man on to his donkey
and took him to an inn where he
looked after him all night.

Next morning the Samaritan had to go on with his journey. He gave the innkeeper two silver coins.

'Look after him well,' he said. 'If you have to spend more money, I will repay you when I come back.'

'Who do you think really cared for the man who was robbed?' Jesus asked the clever man at the end of his story.

'The one who looked after him!' came the reply. The clever man didn't like admitting it was the Samaritan, one of the Jews' enemies!

But Jesus replied, 'Then you must go and behave in the same way.'

# JESUS THE FRIEND

## Keeping the Sabbath

Most people enjoyed listening to Jesus' stories and finding out more about God, but the priests were angry. They were afraid that Jesus was going to upset their laws.

One Saturday Jesus and his friends were walking through the cornfields. Saturday was the day which the Jews set aside to worship God. It was a special, holy day when no work could be done. The leaders had made up all sorts of rules about how the day should be spent.

Jesus and his friends felt hungry and they picked some ears of wheat as they walked along so that they could eat the nutty kernels. Some of the leaders came over to Jesus at once.

'Your friends are breaking the law! No one is allowed to work on the Sabbath! Picking ears of wheat is work!' they cried.

Jesus was angry. He knew that God wanted the Sabbath to be a happy day when people could worship him. The leaders had

invented so many rules that keeping them was a burden. Jesus tried to explain this to the leaders, but they were angry too and would not listen.

'Jesus keeps breaking our laws,' they muttered. They put their heads together and began to plot against Jesus.

One Saturday Jesus went into a synagogue to pray. There he saw a man with a crippled hand. The Jewish leaders watched closely. If Jesus healed the man it would count as work and he would have

broken the law.

Jesus knew what they were thinking.

'When your sheep falls into a hole, you rescue it at once, even on the Sabbath,' he said.

Then he turned to the man.

'Stretch out your hand,' he ordered.

The man obeyed, and at once his hand was well and strong again.

The Jewish leaders were shocked and angry. They began to plot even harder to have Jesus killed.

### Jesus helps a Roman soldier

The synagogue in Capernaum had been built for the Jewish people by a Roman officer. He was a good, just man who believed in God. He had a servant whom he treated well and liked very much. One day the servant grew ill. How worried his master was! He decided to ask Jesus for help.

'Yes, I'll come and make your servant well,' said Jesus.

'No,' replied the officer. 'I don't deserve to have you in my house, and you don't need to come. I know you are under God's authority, just as I am under my commander's. I give orders too, and my soldiers obey me at once. Just give the order and my servant will recover!'

Jesus was amazed.

'I have never met any of my people who believe like this foreigner!' he exclaimed. 'Go home. What you have believed will indeed happen.'

At that very moment the servant became well.

268

### Jesus calms a storm

One evening Jesus and his friends wanted to find a quiet place away from the crowds so that they could rest and spend time together. They decided to take a fishing boat, and set off across the Sea of Galilee. Jesus was tired and he soon fell fast asleep. Suddenly a fierce wind blew up, making huge waves that crashed over the sides of the boat. Jesus' friends were terrified because they were fishermen and they knew how dangerous sudden storms could be. They woke Jesus at once. He stood up and looked around. He saw the tremendous waves, but he wasn't afraid.

'Be still!' he told the storm.

At once the wind dropped and the waves grew calm. His friends were amazed at his power.

'Who can this man really be?' they asked one another. 'Even the wind and sea obey him!'

### Jesus feeds five thousand people

It was always difficult for Jesus and his friends to get away from the crowds to rest. People would even chase after a fishing boat if they caught sight of Jesus on board. As soon as he landed they gathered about him.

Once, when this happened, Jesus felt so sorry for the people that he stayed with them all day. When evening came everyone was hungry.

'Whatever will they find to eat?' asked Andrew, one of Jesus' friends. 'We'd better send them away to the villages to buy food.'

'Give them food yourselves!' said Jesus. 'How much bread do you have?'

'There's a boy here who has five loaves and two fishes,' replied Andrew, 'but they won't go very far in this crowd!'

Quietly Jesus took the basket the boy held out to him.

'Make the people sit down,' he told his friends.

Then he thanked God for the food. He broke the loaves into pieces and divided the fish. His friends began to share the food out among the people, and although there were five thousand in the crowd, there was more than enough for everybody. In fact, after they had finished eating, Jesus' friends filled twelve baskets with the bits that were left over.

Everyone was amazed at Jesus' power.

Some of the people wanted to make Jesus king, but he knew that was not what God wanted. He tried to make his friends understand that the work God had given him to do would be very different.

'My enemies will arrest me and kill me,' he warned them, 'but God will bring me back to life.'

### Jesus helps ten sick men

Jesus and his friends were making their way through the countryside near Samaria. They had just arrived at a village when they saw ten men standing by themselves at a safe distance from everyone else. The men were ill with a terrible skin disease, and people were afraid that if they came too close they might catch it, too. The ten men begged Jesus to make them well, and he told them to go and show a priest that they were better. This was what the law said they had to do if they were cured. As soon as the men started off they became well again. Full of excitement, nine of the men rushed on their way to the priest, but one, who was a Samaritan, turned

back, praising God. He found Jesus and thanked him for making him well so that he no longer needed to hide away from everyone.

'There were ten of you, and you, the foreigner, are the only one who has come back to say thank you!' exclaimed Jesus. 'Go back home,' he told the happy man. 'Your faith has made you completely well again.'

### Jesus and the children

Some families decided to bring their children to see Jesus. When they arrived, Jesus' friends tried to turn them away.

'Jesus is too busy to talk to children!' they said. Jesus heard this and he was angry.

'Don't send the children away!' he called. 'Let them come to me!'

The children crowded round him happily and Jesus put his arms round them. He turned to the grown-ups.

'You need to have faith like these children,' he told them. He touched the children and prayed that God would bless them.

### Jesus and the rich young man

Jesus and his friends were saying goodbye to the children when a young man pushed eagerly through the crowd. Unlike many of the people who came to see Jesus, he looked well fed and well dressed. His beard was carefully cut and combed. He had rings on his fingers and jewels round his neck. Yet there was something the rich man needed. He wanted to go to heaven when he died.

'What must I do?' he asked Jesus.

'You must keep God's laws,' answered Jesus.

'I have obeyed them all my life, Teacher!'

Jesus looked very lovingly at the young man.

'There is still one thing. Sell everything you have. Give the money to the poor and follow me!'

Jesus spoke warmly, but the young man shook his head. He couldn't bring himself to give up his money. Sadly he walked away.

### Jesus and the little tax-collector

However, there was another rich man who wanted to meet Jesus. He was the chief tax-collector of Jericho and his name was Zacchaeus. One day Zacchaeus heard that Jesus was coming to Jericho. At once he rushed down the road to join the crowd who were waiting for Jesus.

Zacchaeus was short and dumpy. He couldn't see over the other people, and he knew that no one would make way for him because he was a tax-collector and a cheat. He charged everyone too much and kept the extra money for himself.

Suddenly he spotted a big tree growing beside the road. Hoping that no one was looking, he clambered up into the branches. Now he had a splendid view of Jesus when he passed underneath!

Zacchaeus had heard that Jesus made friends with tax-collectors, but he couldn't believe it when Jesus looked up into the tree and called his name.

'Come down, Zacchaeus! I must stay at your home today!'

Joyfully, Zacchaeus scrambled down the tree, never minding who saw.

He gave Jesus a splendid welcome, but the crowd followed him to his house grumbling, 'What's Jesus doing, mixing with someone like Zacchaeus?'

Suddenly their grumbles changed to loud cheering. Zacchaeus had started giving his things away.

'Come on, everyone!' he shouted. 'Help yourselves! Have I cheated anyone here? Take this then. Take four times as much!'

When he went back inside, his house seemed bare, but Jesus was there, smiling and pleased.

'Well done,' he said to Zacchaeus, and Zacchaeus felt very happy. He knew that he belonged to God now, and that God had forgiven him all the wrong he had done.

### Jesus and the blind beggar

A blind beggar called Bartimaeus lived in Jericho, too. He was sitting by the roadside as usual, asking the passersby for money when he heard a huge crowd come tramping along. Their feet scuffed up the dust and sent it swirling round the blind man.

'What's happening?' he called out.

'Jesus is coming,' cried the crowd.

At once blind Bartimaeus began to shout, 'Help me, Jesus! Help me!'

Unkind people in the crowd told him to be quiet, but Bartimaeus went on yelling. Then someone said, 'Get up! Jesus heard you shouting. He wants you to come to him.'

Bartimaeus jumped up. He tottered forward to Jesus, his knobbly fingers stretched out in front of him to guide him along.

'What do you want me to do for you?' asked Jesus.

'Oh, Teacher, I want to see!' gasped Bartimaeus, breathlessly.

'Then see!' said Jesus. 'Your faith has made you well.'

The blind man blinked. He looked up, and the first thing he saw was the face of Jesus. Joyfully he followed him along the road, gazing round him at everything and shouting loud praises to God.

### Jesus and the two sisters

Jesus had two special friends who often invited him to stay with them. They were two sisters called Martha and Mary. One day, when Jesus was visiting them, Martha was very busy cleaning and cooking, but Mary sat down beside Jesus and listened to him.

Poor Martha felt very upset.

'Make my sister come and help me with the work!' she said to Jesus.

But he replied, 'Martha, Martha, you are worried and anxious about your work in the kitchen, but Mary has her work to do as well, learning about God, and that is best!'

### Jesus raises Lazarus

Martha and Mary had a brother called Lazarus. One day Lazarus became seriously ill, and within two days he was dead. Jesus was far away at the time, but the two sisters sent someone to him with the news.

By the time Jesus arrived at Bethany where the family lived, Lazarus had been buried. Martha came out to meet Jesus.

'If you had been here, my brother would not have died,' she said, 'but I know that God will do whatever you ask him.

'Martha,' said Jesus, 'everyone who believes in me will rise again from death. Do you believe this?'

'Yes,' she answered him firmly. 'Yes, I believe what you say; you are the Son of God.'

Then Mary came out to Jesus. She too was sure that he could have healed her brother. She was crying bitterly, and so were Lazarus' friends who came with her. Jesus felt very sad. As he walked with them to the place

where Lazarus was buried he began to cry, too.

The body had been wrapped in linen cloths and laid in a cave which had been closed up with a huge, round stone. Jesus told them to remove the stone. Then he prayed to God and called loudly, 'Lazarus, come out!'

At once, Lazarus appeared at the entrance of the cave, alive, but still wrapped in linen cloths.

'Unwind these cloths and let him go,' said Jesus.

Now many more people believed in him, but the priests were furious. They wanted more than ever to have Jesus killed, and they watched him carefully, waiting for a chance to seize him.

## THE EASTER STORY

### *Jesus goes to Jerusalem*

Jesus knew very well that his life was in danger, but he knew, too, that it was God's plan for him to die and come to life again. So he set off firmly for Jerusalem, to celebrate the Passover Festival there, even though the city would be full of his enemies.

As they made their way towards the city, Jesus had a surprise for two of his friends.

'You remember our holy writings say that the king whom God is sending will ride into Jerusalem on a donkey? You'll find a donkey in the next village. Untie him and bring him to me. If anyone asks, say, "the Master needs him," and they will let you take him.'

Full of excitement the two friends ran off.

They found the donkey easily, and started to untie his rope.

'Hey! Stop!' a man shouted from a doorway. 'What are you doing, taking that donkey?'

'The Master needs him!' said the friends, as Jesus had told them.

'Oh, well, that's different!' said the man. 'Treat him carefully, won't you? No one has ever ridden him before, but if Jesus wants him, he can have him.'

They untied the donkey and led him to Jesus.

Crowds of people were flocking to Jerusalem for the Passover Festival. Everybody was happy because of the holiday, and when they saw Jesus they cheered with excitement. 'Here comes the king!' they shouted.

They cut down palm branches from the trees and waved them in the air. Some people even spread their cloaks in the road, and the donkey walked over them as he carried Jesus slowly into the city. On through the narrow streets they went, to the beautiful temple where Jews from all over the world gathered to praise God.

### Jesus clears the temple

At once Jesus saw something that made him very angry.

The temple courtyard was like a market place, where people could buy birds and animals to offer to God. Lambs bleated loudly, and white doves cooed in cages.

Special coins had to be used inside the temple area, so every-one had to change their money, just as though they were going to a foreign country. The money changers were cheats and kept most of the change. So Jesus seized hold of a whip and drove them out.

He toppled over their tables. Coins rolled in all directions. Then the temple was in an uproar! Doves flew free. Sheep butted one another and calves mooed, while the dealers yelled and raged.

'God wants his temple to be a quiet place where people can pray to him!' cried Jesus. 'You dealers are wrong! You have made God's temple like a robber's den! Get out!'

The priests and leaders, who hated Jesus, were furious with him. It was their job to keep order in the temple. So they tried to trap him with a trick question.

'Teacher,' they said politely, 'should we pay taxes to the Romans or not?'

If Jesus said, 'no', he would be in trouble with the Romans. If he said 'yes', the people would be angry, for the Jews hated having to pay taxes and obey the Roman law. His friends waited anxiously to see what he would do.

'Let me see a coin,' he said. 'Whose name and head are stamped on it?'

'The Roman Emperor's,' they replied.

'Then pay the Roman Emperor what is his, and pay God what belongs to him,' answered Jesus.

Silenced, they slunk away, but Jesus knew that they still watched him closely.

## Jesus and the expensive perfume

Every day for the next week Jesus taught the crowds in the temple, but at night, for safety, he and his friends left Jerusalem to stay in a little village close by. One evening a woman called Mary Magdalene came to find Jesus. She brought a jar of expensive perfume and she loved Jesus so much that she poured the whole jar over his

## Jesus and the poor widow

As they walked about the temple, Jesus and his friends saw rich people dropping silver coins into the collecting boxes. Then they noticed a poor woman. She was a widow with no family to help her, and it was plain that she never had enough to eat. She dropped two small copper coins into the box.

'Look, friends,' said Jesus, 'this poor woman has put in far more than all the rich people we have seen.'

'Has she?' his friends asked, amazed.

'Yes,' Jesus answered. 'You see they gave God only what they thought they could spare. They have plenty of money left, but she is so poor she had only those two coins. She has given God all the money she had.'

head and feet. A wonderful scent filled the room. Mary's tears fell on Jesus' feet as she kissed them and wiped them with her hair.

'What a waste!' said Judas, one of Jesus' followers. 'Mary could have sold this perfume and given the money to the poor.'

'No,' replied Jesus. 'Mary has done a beautiful thing for me before I die.'

## Jesus and Judas

Mary was glad, but Judas scowled angrily at Jesus' words. He looked after the money for Jesus and the others and he used to help himself from their supply. If Mary had sold her perfume there would have been more for him to steal. Now, every day, he grew greedier for money and he began to be angry with Jesus because he cared for different things. At last he went to the priests.

'What will you give me if I help you to capture Jesus?' he asked.

They counted thirty silver coins into his hand. Judas slipped away, but he was watchful now, waiting for a time when Jesus was alone and his enemies could capture him without any trouble.

## The Passover meal

Towards the end of the week the time came for the Passover which the Jews celebrated with a special supper of flat bread and lamb with sauce and herbs. Jesus found a secret room in Jerusalem where he could eat the Passover meal in safety with his friends. As they sat at the table Jesus stood up and took off his long tunic. He tied a towel round his waist, poured water into a bowl, and went round his friends in turn, washing the dust of the city streets from their feet.

Simon Peter said, 'Lord, you mustn't wash my feet like a servant!'

'I'm washing your feet because I love you, Peter,' said Jesus. 'My friends, I am happy to work for you like a servant. You must be ready, too, to serve one another in humble ways.'

Jesus sat down again. 'One of you is going to hand me over to my enemies,' he said sadly.

'Who could it be?' they wondered anxiously, but Judas knew. Quietly he slipped outside. Then Jesus took some bread, broke it and shared it with his friends.

'This is my body, which is given for you,' he said. 'When you break and eat bread together like this, you must remember me.'

Sad and puzzled, they shared the bread.

Then Jesus passed the cup of wine round among them.

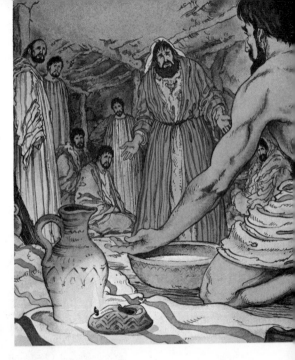

'Drink this, all of you,' he said. 'This is my blood, which will be poured out so that everyone's sins can be forgiven by God.'

### Judas betrays Jesus

They did not understand. Why did he keep talking about dying when every day crowds followed him and praised him? Sadly they left the room and went with him to a quiet garden outside the city where Jesus liked to pray.

On the way Jesus warned them yet again of all that was to happen.

'I'll stick by you,' declared Simon Peter. 'Even if all the others run away and leave you.'

'Before you hear the cock crow tomorrow morning you will say three times that you do not know me,' said Jesus. 'Wait here, all of you,' he added. 'Don't go to sleep. Stay awake and pray for me.'

Then he went further into the garden and prayed alone: 'Father, if it is possible, don't let me die this horrible death!'

His hair stuck to his forehead, wet with sweat. With a great effort he cried out, 'Father, don't do what I want. Do what you know is best.'

He returned to his friends and

found them asleep.

'Could you not stay awake?' asked Jesus. 'Get up now. Here come my enemies.'

Into the quiet garden came Judas, followed by the temple police and a rough crowd, armed with sticks and spears. The chief priests had sent them all to capture Jesus.

'The man I kiss is the one you want,' muttered Judas to the police.

He went straight to Jesus. 'Peace, Teacher,' Judas said, and kissed him.

Jesus looked steadily at Judas. 'Why are you here, friend?' he asked gently. 'Have you come to give me away with your kiss?'

### Jesus is arrested

Then the soldiers grabbed Jesus and held him securely.

'Don't hurt my friends,' Jesus warned them.

Simon Peter had a sword hidden under his cloak. He wanted to defend Jesus, and he struck at a slave and cut off the man's ear.

'Put your sword away, Simon,' said Jesus. 'I shall go with them willingly, for this is the way my Father has chosen for me.'

The crowd fell silent.

'Did you have to come with sticks and spears to capture me?'

Jesus asked them. 'Day after day I went to the temple. You all saw me there, but none of you arrested me then.'

He knew that they had been afraid to arrest him because of the crowds. He touched the wounded man and healed his ear.

'Now is the time for the powers of darkness to have their way,' Jesus said.

The soldiers hurried him roughly out of the garden. His terrified friends scattered among the trees, leaving Jesus alone in the power of the men who wanted to kill him because they thought that he broke God's Law.

Now that they had managed to capture Jesus at last, his enemies had to find a reason to have him killed. All night long they asked him questions. The leaders brought in people who told lies about Jesus but none of their stories agreed.

Finally, at down, the high priest asked, 'Are you the Son of God?'

'Yes, I am,' Jesus replied.

'He claims to be God! That's against our holy law!' cried the high priest.

'He's guilty!' the others agreed. 'He must die!'

### Peter lets Jesus down

Outside, in the courtyard, there was a fire where the soldiers and the leaders' servants could warm themselves while they waited.

Simon Peter had slipped in with the crowd that came with Jesus, and he went and stood by the fire.

The high priest's servants noticed him.

'Weren't you one of Jesus' friends?' asked a girl.

'Oh, no, I don't even know him,' declared Simon Peter uneasily, but a little later one of the men spotted the strong fisherman.

'Hey, this fellow's one of them, too!' he said.

'Me? Certainly not!' lied Simon Peter.

'Come on, you can't fool us! You're from Galilee, too. Your accent gives you away. Of course you were with Jesus.'

'No, I don't know him!' Simon Peter shouted.

Beyond the courtyard the first pale streaks of daylight showed in the sky. A cock close by crowed loudly. Then Simon Peter remembered what Jesus had told him – that before the cock crowed in the morning he would say three times that he did not know Jesus.

Peter rushed outside and cried bitterly.

### Jesus and the Roman governor

The Jewish leaders were not allowed to put people to death. Only the Roman rulers could do that. So Jesus was sent to the Roman governor, a man called Pontius Pilate.

'We've brought you a real trouble-maker,' the priests warned Pilate. 'He stirs up our people against the Romans. He even calls himself a king!''

Pilate looked at Jesus curiously. 'Are you a king?' he asked.

'So you say,' answered Jesus, and he would not reply to any more of Pilate's questions.

Pilate looked helplessly at his prisoner. He knew that Jesus had done nothing that deserved death, but he knew that the priests wanted him killed. Pilate did not want to annoy the priests. He had an idea.

He led Jesus outside and showed him to the crowd which was waiting there.

'You know I always free one of your prisoners at Passover time,' Pilate told the crowd. 'Here is Jesus. Shall I let him go?'

'No!' shouted the people. Then someone yelled, 'Free Barabbas instead!' and other voices joined in, although Barabbas was a bandit.

Pilate was afraid of the angry crowd, so he had Barabbas set free and handed Jesus over to the Roman soldiers, who beat him cruelly. They made a crown from thorny twigs and forced it on to Jesus' head. Then they wrapped a purple cloak round him and bowed to him, jeering, 'Long live the king!'

At last Pilate took Jesus out to the crowd again. 'Here is your king,' he said. 'What do you want me to do with him? He has done nothing to deserve death.'

But the priests had persuaded the people that Jesus ought to die, and the crowd yelled, 'The cross! Let him die on the cross!'

It was the same crowd who had welcomed him to the city only five days before.

### Jesus is crucified

So Jesus was led away to die. He had to carry his own cross, but his shoulders were torn and bleeding from the soldiers' whips, and he stumbled and fell under the weight. So the soldiers seized a man called Simon, who had come from Cyrene in North Africa to keep the festival in Jerusalem, and forced him to carry Jesus' heavy load. Simon remembered that cross for the rest of his life.

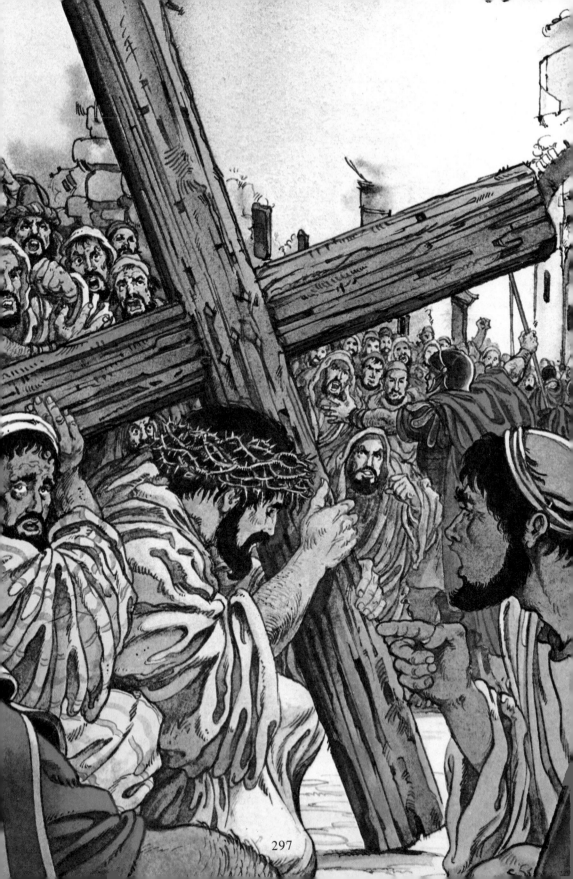

Beyond the city walls was a place called 'Skull Hill'. There the Roman soldiers laid Jesus down on the cross and hammered nails through his hands and feet.

Jesus said, 'Father, forgive them. They don't understand what they are doing.'

Two robbers were nailed to crosses on either side of him.

Some of the soldiers played dice to pass the time. The winner would have for his prize the clothes which Jesus had worn. A large crowd watched Jesus, and their leaders jeered, 'Get yourself off the cross, king!'

One of the robbers joined in, but the other said, 'We are both getting what we deserve, but this man hasn't done anything wrong!' Turning his head towards Jesus he said, 'Remember me when you come back as king.'

'Today you shall be in Paradise with me,' Jesus answered firmly.

It was nine o'clock when they nailed Jesus to the cross. At midday the sky grew black. Jesus called out into the darkness, 'My God, my God, why have you deserted me?'

Some people heard him and wondered if, even now, God would rescue him, but nothing happened.

Jesus had only a little strength left. 'I'm so thirsty!' he gasped.

Soldiers soaked a sponge with sour wine and lifted it up to moisten his lips.

'Everything is finished,' Jesus cried. He bowed his head and died.

## Jesus is alive

Two of his secret followers begged Pilate for Jesus' body. They wrapped it in strips of linen cloth and took it to a garden where there was a new grave cut in the rock. Some of the women who had been Jesus' friends too, followed the men to the garden. They watched while the men rolled a heavy stone in front of the entrance to the grave, and they all went home very sadly. The holy

Magdalene made her way to the garden. With a shock she saw that the grave stood wide open. She ran to fetch Simon Peter and another friend, John.

The two men raced to the grave. It was quite empty. There was no body at all. Only the linen cloths lay on the ground. Puzzled, the men went away, but Mary stayed by the grave, crying. She did not see a man standing close by. 'What is the matter? Why are you crying?' the man asked her. She thought he must be the gardener. 'Sir,' she said, 'they've moved his body. Do you know where it's been taken?'

'Mary!' said the man, and suddenly she recognised him. It was Jesus!

'Master!' she exclaimed happily, drying her tears.

'Go and tell my friends I am alive,' said Jesus joyfully.

Mary ran back at once to Jesus' friends, but they wouldn't believe her.

'Alive? It can't be true!' they muttered.

Sabbath was just beginning, so they could do no work, but as soon as Saturday evening came, the women began preparing perfumes and spices to lay in the linen grave cloths. It was the only way they could show how much they cared for Jesus.

Early on Sunday morning Mary

### A walk to Emmaus

That afternoon two of the men left Jerusalem for a nearby village called Emmaus. As they walked together along the road, talking to each other, a stranger caught up with them.

'What are you discussing?' he asked.

'Haven't you heard about Jesus of Nazareth?' they said. 'We thought he was the one sent by God to help us, but he has been put to death. Now some women are saying he is alive again. Certainly his body has disappeared. It's very puzzling.'

'But don't our holy writings say that God's promised king must die and rise again?' asked the stranger, and he explained many things to them as they walked along.

When they arrived at Emmaus it was getting dark and they asked him to stay with them. So he went to their house and shared their

supper. He took the bread, thanked God and broke it, just as Jesus used to do. Then they saw he *was* Jesus. They were overjoyed, but he disappeared immediately.

The two men rushed straight back to Jerusalem. They wanted to tell the others, but their friends had their own exciting news to tell. 'Jesus is alive! Simon Peter saw him, too!'

'We know he's alive. He met us on the road and talked to us!' the two men answered.

### Jesus meets his friends

Suddenly Jesus was in the room with them. They were terrified for they thought he must be a ghost. Quickly Jesus spoke to them.

'I'm no ghost. Touch me. You can't touch a ghost!'

Still they could hardly believe it. Yet there he was, showing them the marks in his hands and feet where he had been nailed to the cross.

'Have you any food, friends?' he asked.

They gave him some fish, and watched, amazed, as he ate.

'Soon you must go and tell everyone that I died and came alive again so that their sins could be forgiven,' Jesus told them. 'But you must wait here in Jerusalem until God sends the Holy Spirit to be with you in my place. He will give you the help you need.'

### Jesus and Thomas

One of Jesus' friends, Thomas, was out when Jesus met the others. He didn't believe their news.

'Unless I actually touch the scars in his hands, I won't believe Jesus is alive!' Thomas said.

Eight days later Thomas was with the others and Jesus came again.

'Look, Thomas,' he said, 'here are the marks of the nails. Touch these scars and believe.'

Thomas fell to his knees. 'You are my Lord and my God!' he declared.

'Thomas, you believe because you can see me,' said Jesus, 'but how happy people will be who believe in me without seeing me!'

## Jesus and Peter

Later on, some of Jesus' friends went home to Galilee, back to their fishing. One night they went out in their boat, but they didn't catch a single fish. At daybreak someone on the shore shouted to them, 'Throw out your net to the right!'

They tossed the net out, and at once it was weighed down with fish.

'That's Jesus!' John said to Simon Peter.

Simon leapt into the sea and swam to Jesus. On the beach Jesus had a fire blazing and some fish ready cooked.

'Bring some more fish,' he said. Simon Peter went back and hauled the heavy net ashore.

'Breakfast's ready!' Jesus called.

After breakfast Jesus asked Simon Peter quietly, three times, 'Simon, do you love me?'

'Yes, Lord,' answered Simon

Peter each time, remembering sadly how he had lied three times about Jesus.

'Then look after my followers,' said Jesus. Now Simon Peter knew that Jesus still trusted him.

### Jesus goes back to Heaven

Soon the time came for Jesus to leave his friends and go back to heaven to be with God. One day he and his close friends went out of the city. They climbed a hill. Jesus prayed that his friends would always know God's love and peace, and he gave them a

command: 'You must tell everyone the good news,' Jesus said. 'Remember, I am alive for ever and I shall be with you always, right to the end of time, just as I told you.'

Then he disappeared from their sight. They would not see him again on earth, but they knew the Holy Spirit would come and help them.

They went back to Jerusalem and they started going to the temple every day to thank God for Jesus. They knew that God had sent him to die and come to life again so that everyone who believed in him could be freed from the power of wrong-doing, death and evil.

'Jesus is alive!' they sang, knowing that from then on the whole world would be different.

# THE FIRST CHRISTIANS

### *The new helper*

One morning, six weeks later, Jesus' friends met together to pray as usual. Suddenly the roar of a rushing wind filled the room where they were sitting. Leaping flames touched their heads, and they felt that God was very close to them. The special helper, God's Holy Spirit, had come, just as Jesus had promised. They began to praise God excitedly and at once they found themselves speaking in different languages, which God's Holy Spirit made them able to do. Still praising God, they ran out into the street.

The sound of their laughter and happy shouts soon drew a crowd round them. People from many foreign countries had come to Jerusalem for the Jewish festival of Pentecost. They were amazed to hear Jesus' friends talking about God in their own languages. Some people tried to turn it into a joke.

'These men are drunk!' they jeered. 'That's why they're shouting and talking like this!'

'No!' Peter declared firmly. 'We're not drunk, how could we be? It's far too early in the morning! God has sent us his Spirit and now we can tell you about Jesus. Jesus is God's Son and you put him to death here in Jerusalem. But God has brought him back to life, just as he promised in our holy writings.'

When the people heard what Peter said they were frightened and sorry. 'What must we do?' they asked.

'If you believe in Jesus you must stop doing wrong,' replied Peter. 'Then be baptised in his name, and God will forgive you. He will give you his Holy Spirit to help you to do things that please him.'

'We must do what Peter says,' many agreed. About three thousand people decided to be baptised that day. They too were strengthened by the power of the Holy Spirit and they listened eagerly as Peter and the others taught them more about Jesus.

Because they knew that God had forgiven them, and given them the Holy Spirit to help them to please him, the new followers of Jesus felt very happy. They all shared everything they had. They met in one another's houses to eat their meals and pray together. Every day they went to the temple to praise God, and they were so full of joy that more and more people kept joining them.

### Peter and John heal a lame man

One day Peter and his friend John were going into the temple when they met a lame beggar. He used to sit beside one of the temple gates all day, calling, 'Give me some money! I've never walked in all my life. Give me a coin so that I can buy food!'

Peter and John stopped, and the beggar watched them hopefully.

'I have no money to give you,' Peter said, 'but I shall give you what I have. In the name of Jesus I command you: get up and walk!'

He helped the beggar to stand. At once the man felt strength flow into his weak feet and ankles. He let go of Peter's hand and started to walk. Soon he was jumping and leaping into the air shouting, 'Look, I can walk! I can really move about! How good God is! Thank you, God! You've made me able to walk like everyone else after I'd been lame all my life.'

He ran into the temple where everyone who knew him was amazed to see him walking about, praising God.

## Peter and John in trouble

Peter explained to the people in the temple that it was the power of Jesus that had made the lame man walk again. Some of the priests overheard and were furious. They thought they had got rid of Jesus! They actually had Peter and John arrested and kept in prison overnight. In spite of this, many of the people who saw what happened to the lame man became followers of Jesus, too.

Next day all the Jewish leaders, including the high priest, met together and questioned Peter and John.

'Where did you get the power to make a lame man walk?' the high priest demanded.

'We healed the man in the name of Jesus,' Peter explained. Then the Holy Spirit helped him to add bravely, 'You ordered Jesus to be put to death, but God brought him back to life, and now Jesus is the only one who can save us and help us!'

The leaders listened in amazement.
'What shall we do?'
they said to one another.
'We can't punish men
who healed a lame
man! It's the talk of
Jerusalem already! But
we must stop this new
faith before more
people stop worshipping
God in our way and

start following Jesus.'

So they told the two friends never to use the name of Jesus again.

'You are our leaders,' Peter and John replied, 'but God comes first, and we must do what he wants — we just can't stop telling everyone about Jesus!'

The leaders could say no more. They had to let Peter and John go.

Quickly the two made their way back to their friends. Together they all prayed that God would make them brave enough to go on talking about Jesus, no matter what the rulers threatened to do.

## More trouble

God answered their prayers, and more and more people believed in Jesus. Crowds flocked in from the country, bringing sick friends with them and they were all made well.

The high priest and his followers were so angry that they had Peter and John arrested again and locked up in prison. That night

God sent an angel to their cell.

'Go back to the temple. Stand where everyone can see you, and tell them about Jesus,' said the angel, unlocking the barred gates.

Peter and John obeyed at once. When the high priest got up next morning and sent his men to the prison no one could find the prisoners! While they were wondering what could have happened and checking all the locks, a man rushed in: 'Those men you locked up last night are standing in the temple this very minute teaching everyone about Jesus,' he said breathlessly.

The high priest sent for them at once.

'We ordered you not to teach about Jesus,' the high priest thundered, but Peter answered boldly, 'We must do what God wants. He brought Jesus back to life, and we must tell people what he has done!'

When the priests heard this, they wanted to put Peter and his friends to death, but one of the leaders, a wise teacher called Gamaliel, whom everyone respected, advised them to be careful.

'If this new faith is just a made-up story, it will soon fade away and be forgotten. But if it is from God nothing you can do will stop it. Be careful! You might find yourselves fighting against God!'

So the priests had Peter and John beaten and then let them go. The friends were glad that God had let them suffer because they believed in Jesus. They took no notice of the priests but kept on telling everyone their good news.

### Stephen

The new group of Jesus' followers soon had some other problems to face. Although they were all Jewish, they came from different countries and some spoke Jewish languages while others spoke only Greek. Some families were rich, but most were very poor. Every day they shared out their food, but the Greek-speaking families began to complain that they weren't getting enough. At last Peter and his ten friends, who had been the first followers of Jesus, called the whole group together.

'Choose seven men whom you know are wise and full of God's Holy Spirit, and put them in

charge of the money and the food supplies. Then everyone will get all they need,' they said.

One of the men who was chosen was called Stephen. He loved Jesus so much that he was able to do many wonderful things for the sick and needy people. He spoke so bravely about Jesus that the priests and leaders noticed and became his enemies.

Young Jewish men used to go to Jerusalem to learn more about the law from the priests. One young student called Saul heard about the followers of Jesus. Like the priests, he decided that they were wrong and ought to be stopped. One day Saul heard Stephen teaching in a synagogue, telling everyone that Jesus was alive.

'Jesus is with God now,' Stephen declared, 'but he is still helping us to lead lives which please God.'

Saul stared angrily at Stephen. 'This man must be stopped!' he hissed to a friend who was with him. 'Stephen and the others who follow Jesus are spoiling the way we Jews have tried to worship and please God for hundreds of years!'

Saul's friend nodded. Other Jewish leaders agreed with Saul. They made a plot to arrest Stephen. Soon he was on trial for his life.

Stephen faced his judges fearlessly. 'We can read in our holy writings that God sent to our people teachers to show us how to please him. Now in our time he has sent us his own Son, Jesus, but you still wouldn't listen. Instead you killed him!'

'And we'll kill you, too!' they snarled, but Stephen looked up and his eyes shone.

'I see Jesus in heaven with God, sharing his power!' he cried.

At this, they dragged him out of the city. They tossed their cloaks to Saul so that their arms were free to pick up heavy stones and hurl them at Stephen. Badly wounded, Stephen managed to pray, 'Lord Jesus, take me to you. Don't blame them for this, Lord!'

Saul listened angrily. He was glad to see Stephen die.

It was no longer safe to be a follower of Jesus. Saul and his friends wanted to destroy the new faith completely. Believers were dragged off to prison and punished. Many of them were forced to leave Jerusalem, but wherever they went they told people about Jesus, and the new faith spread all over the country.

### Philip in Samaria

One man, called Philip, went to Samaria telling everyone there about Jesus. They were all amazed when they saw lame people walk and evil spirits driven away through the power of Jesus.

Philip baptised all the people who wanted to follow Jesus. There were so many new believers that Peter and John came over from Jerusalem to meet them. They prayed for the new believers to receive the Holy Spirit, too, so that they could have his power to help them to serve God.

### The Ethiopian treasurer

At about this time, a very important man was on his way home from Jerusalem. He was the Queen of Ethiopia's treasurer. He loved God and wanted to learn more about him. As he rode home in his chariot he was reading from the Bible. God guided Philip to him, and he ran up to the treasurer's chariot. When Philip saw that the man was reading the Bible, he asked him if he understood it.

'How can I, without someone to help me?' replied the Ethiopian. He invited Philip to get into the chariot with him and explain the chapter he was reading. Philip agreed, and as he explained the chapter he told the treasurer about Jesus.

After a little while they drove past a pool of water. 'I believe everything you have told me,' said the treasurer, 'and look! There's some water! Can't you baptise me now, so that I can be a follower of Jesus, too?'

They got out of the chariot and Philip baptised him. Then the treasurer drove home happily, eager to tell his friends in Ethiopia about his new faith.

Meanwhile, Saul went on attacking everyone in Jerusalem who followed Jesus. He realised that the new faith was growing in other towns too, so he asked the high priest to let him go to the city of Damascus to arrest the believers there as well.

'I'll drag them back here in chains!' shouted Saul.

The high priest gave him permission, and Saul set out for Damascus. Suddenly, as he was riding along, a dazzling light shone in his eyes. Blinded, he fell to the ground. Then he heard a voice speaking to him: 'Saul, Saul, why are you attacking me?'

'Who are you, Lord?' Saul asked, amazed.

'I am Jesus,' came the answer. 'When you attack my followers you attack me, too. Get up now and go into Damascus. You will be told what to do there.'

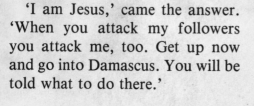

The men who were travelling with Saul heard the voice, but could see no one. They watched as Saul stood up uncertainly. He was completely blind and they had to lead him into Damascus.

For three days he stayed in a house there without eating or drinking anything, spending the whole time in prayer. Meanwhile, the Lord Jesus was preparing someone to help him. A man called Ananias saw Jesus in a dream.

'Go and help Saul,' said Jesus. 'He is staying in Straight Street.'

'Oh no, Lord, I've heard about that man,' answered Ananias. 'He's our worst enemy!'

'Go and help him,' Jesus repeated. 'I have chosen him to tell people all over the world about me.'

So Ananias went to Saul and laid his hands on his head. 'Brother, Saul, the Lord Jesus sent me to you. He wants you to see again.'

At once something like fish scales fell from Saul's eyes and he could see. He asked to be baptised straightaway as a sign that he followed Jesus. Only then did he have something to eat.

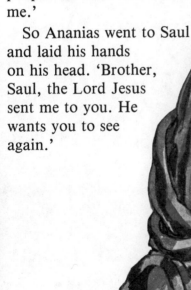

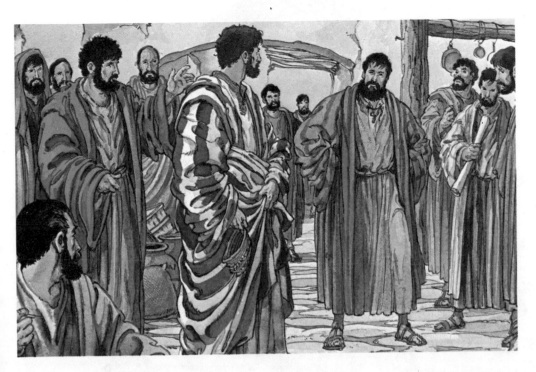

### Saul escapes from Damascus

Saul stayed in Damascus and visited all the synagogues in the city. He told everyone what had happened to him.

'I know now that Jesus is the Son of God,' he said.

Many people who heard him came to believe, too, but others refused to follow Jesus. 'Saul's deserted us and joined those mistaken followers of Jesus,' they said. 'We must kill him before he spreads his story further. Let's keep a watch on all the city gates. He won't be able to sneak out of Damascus now!'

But Saul's new friends made plans, too. One night when it was dark, they hid Saul in a basket and lowered it over the city wall. So Saul escaped and hurried back to Jerusalem to join the other believers there. He hoped it would not be too hard for them to trust him.

At first they *were* afraid to trust Saul, but there was one man, called Barnabas, who did believe his story. He took Saul to the leaders of the group and told them what had happened to him.

'Saul has already risked his life for the Lord Jesus,' Barnabas explained warmly. So at last the believers welcomed Saul. He talked to everyone about Jesus, especially to the men who had planned Stephen's death. They were angry and tried to kill him, too, so his new friends sent him back to his family's home in the large seaport of Tarsus where he would be safe.

## The churches grow

Now there was a time of peace for the followers of Jesus. Arrests and punishments hadn't stopped their faith and in the peaceful time it went on growing. They knew that Jesus was with them, no matter where they went. When they made new friends they told them about Jesus, and soon there were groups of people far and wide

who followed Jesus and loved God. They cared for one another and shared their belongings, just like the first believers in Jerusalem. These groups were called 'churches'. More and more people joined them.

Peter had a busy time now. He left Jerusalem and travelled through all the towns round about. In the town of Lydda he healed a man who had lain in bed, quite unable to move, for eight whole years. After that many more people came to believe in Jesus.

### Dorcas

Near Lydda, in the port of Joppa, there lived a woman called Dorcas, who liked to help poor people because she loved Jesus. One day she grew very ill, and soon she died. When her friends heard, they asked Peter to come to Joppa.

As soon as he arrived, a sad crowd of women showed him the clothes that Dorcas had sewn for them. Peter went up to the room where Dorcas' body lay. He knelt by her bed and prayed. Then he said to the dead woman, 'Dorcas, get up!'

At once Dorcas opened her eyes and sat up. Peter helped her to her feet and called her friends.

The wonderful news spread all over Joppa and many people believed in Jesus. Everybody wanted Peter to tell them more about Jesus, so he agreed to stay on in Joppa.

### Peter's dream

Houses in that part of the world had flat roofs where people could store their belongings, and which they could use as an extra room in hot weather. One day Peter went up on the roof of the house where he was staying in Joppa to pray. While he was there, God gave him a special dream. Peter saw a big sheet coming down from the sky, full of animals. A voice told him to kill an animal for his dinner. At first Peter was pleased because he was hungry, but then he saw that the animals were all of the kind that Jews are forbidden to eat by their law.

'No, Lord,' he said. 'I can't eat that!'

But God told him that everything he had made was good, and again invited him to eat.

At last Peter woke up. He was wondering what his dream meant when some men called to see him. They had been sent by a Roman officer called Cornelius, who wanted Peter to come to his house and tell him about Jesus. Jews were not allowed to mix with foreigners — but Peter remembered his dream. Now he understood that in God's eyes there were no differences between Jews and foreigners. God made them all, just as he made different sorts of animals for food. So Peter went with the men to meet the Roman officer.

## Peter and Cornelius

Cornelius was delighted to see Peter. Although he was a Roman, he loved and worshipped God. He led Peter into his house where his friends and relations were waiting, too, to hear about God and his son Jesus.

'God has shown me that he loves everyone, no matter what race they belong to,' said Peter. He started to tell them about Jesus.

While he was speaking the power of God filled the room and the Holy Spirit came to Cornelius and his friends. They found themselves praising God in other languages, just as Jesus' friends had done in Jerusalem. The Jewish believers from Joppa who had gone with Peter were amazed, but Peter baptised Cornelius and his friends in the name of Jesus.

## Peter in prison

Soon the peaceful time came to an end and trouble started again for the followers of Jesus. In Jerusalem life grew very dangerous, for King Herod Agrippa himself began to help the priests to hunt out the friends of Jesus. Fisherman James, who had left his boat years before to follow Jesus, was killed, and Peter, back from Joppa, was arrested. He was closely guarded by four soldiers.

The followers of Jesus met together to pray for him, and they had a special meeting on the evening before his trial.

That same night Peter was sleeping, chained between two guards. More soldiers guarded the gates. Suddenly a great light shone in his cell. An angel shook Peter awake.

'Get up at once!'

The heavy chains fell from Peter's wrists. He was free! Not sure whether he really was awake or still only dreaming, Peter followed the angel past the sleeping guards. The prison gate opened wide for them and they walked out. Peter found himself alone in the empty street. The cold air convinced him that this was no dream. God had freed him! He ran to find his friends.

Hurriedly he knocked at the door of the house where his friends were still praying for him.

'Who is it?' came the voice of the servant girl, Rhoda.

When she heard Peter reply, she was amazed. She ran to tell the others but they simply would not believe her.

'It's true – he's still knocking!' she cried.

She was so excited that she had forgotten to let him in!

They opened the door and were overjoyed to see that it *was* Peter. He told them how God had rescued him, then he slipped away somewhere safe while his friends praised God and talked together about the wonderful things he was doing for them.

# PAUL THE TRAVELLER

### *Saul goes to Antioch*

Soon the news reached the believers in Jerusalem that a church had started in a town called Antioch. The people there loved Jesus so much that they were always talking about him, and they had been given the nickname, 'the Christians'.

'This is good news,' said the church leaders in Jerusalem. 'Let's send Saul's friend Barnabas to Antioch to help the new believers to learn more about Jesus.'

'Of course I'll go,' said Barnabas. 'But I think I might need some help for this special job.' He went all the way to Tarsus to find Saul.

'Why don't you come and help me to work with the new friends of Jesus in Antioch?' he asked.

Saul agreed gladly. For a whole year Barnabas and Saul worked hard in Antioch, until one special day when God spoke to the Christians as they were praying. 'I want Saul and Barnabas to do something special for me. They must travel far away to many other countries to tell people there about Jesus,' said God.

Full of excitement, all the Christians placed their hands on the two friends and prayed for them. Then they set off on their travels. They took Barnabas' young nephew, John Mark, with them to help them in their work.

## Saul and Elymas

First they sailed to the island of Cyprus where Barnabas had been born. The Roman governor gave them a warm welcome. He wanted to hear about Jesus, but a friend of his, a magician called Elymas, was standing by. He didn't want the governor to believe in Jesus and he kept interrupting Saul. This made Saul angry. He spoke sternly to Elymas.

'Stop trying to twist the truth, you trickster! Because you are setting yourself against God, you will go blind for a while!'

At once Elymas felt as though a thick fog was covering his eyes. He groped around for someone to lead him. The governor was amazed; he felt sure that Saul must be speaking the truth about Jesus.

From now on Saul began to use his Roman name of Paul. But, although he travelled to many other countries, he never forgot his own people, the Jews.

## John Mark goes home

Paul and Barnabas planned to travel into Turkey. John Mark was very quiet on the voyage across from Cyprus. Once they reached the mainland he refused to go any further with them. Perhaps he was homesick, or jealous of Paul who seemed to be getting more important than his uncle, Barnabas.

Rather sadly, Paul and Barnabas went on their way over the high mountain passes to a district called Pisidia. They began to teach the Jews who lived there about Jesus. Many of them listened eagerly and the good news spread like wildfire through the surrounding villages. Even here, the Jewish leaders were angry. 'Those two travellers, Paul and Barnabas, are stirring up trouble in our town,' the leaders told some of the rich citizens, who believed them. Paul and Barnabas were thrown roughly out of the town. But they went bravely on their way. 'God is with us,' Paul said. 'There are groups of Christians everywhere now and the new Christians here will go on meeting together, even though we've been thrown out.' Paul always remembered the new Christians, even when he was far away. He prayed for them and wrote letters to encourage them.

## Jupiter and Mercury

One day Paul and Barnabas came to a city called Lystra, where there was a temple to the chief Roman god, Jupiter. As Paul talked about Jesus he saw a lame man in the crowd. He felt sure that the man believed what he was saying and could be made well.

'Stand up and walk!' ordered Paul.

The man jumped to his feet immediately, completely cured.

'These men must really be gods in disguise!' shouted the crowd.

They decided that Barnabas must be Jupiter because he was the taller, and that Paul must be Mercury, the messenger of the gods, because he did the talking.

The priest of Jupiter brought flowers and bulls to offer to Paul and Barnabas. The two friends were horrified! They ran into the crowd, tearing their clothes and shouting, 'Stop! We're not gods; just ordinary people like you, come to tell you about the one true God who loves you and provides you with the good things you need to live!'

They only just managed to stop the crowd worshipping them!

### Paul and Barnabas disagree

After many adventures the two friends returned home to Antioch. They had been away for two years and had travelled over a thousand miles. Because of their work, many new churches had begun.

The Christians in Antioch were overjoyed to hear that God was giving his help and power to so many new followers of Jesus.

Paul and Barnabas spent some time with them, and then they

decided to set out on another journey to visit all the new churches and see how they were getting on.

Barnabas wanted to take John Mark with them again.

'That wouldn't be right at all!' said Paul sharply. 'He didn't stick it out last time. He deserted us as soon as we set foot in Turkey and had those high mountains to cross!'

'Well, I think we should give him another chance. After all,

the boy is older now . . .' began Barnabas, but Paul refused to agree.

After some argument they decided to go their different ways. Barnabas set sail for Cyprus and took John Mark with him, while Paul chose a new companion called Silas.

### Two new helpers

Paul and Silas revisited the new churches in Turkey. When they reached Lystra they found everyone talking about a young man called Timothy.

'He's such a fine Christian!' they told Paul. 'His mother is Jewish and she's a Christian now, too. His father was a Greek.'

Paul listened thoughtfully.

'I'd like to meet that boy!' he said to Silas. 'We could use someone like him, who belongs to both the Jews and the Greeks!'

When Paul met Timothy he liked him at once. He asked him to join them on their travels. Timothy was delighted, even though he knew it would be difficult and dangerous. He and Paul became very fond of each other, and Paul always treated Timothy just like a son.

Before long another helper joined the three travellers — a Greek doctor called Luke. Luke turned out to be a faithful friend. He also wrote down the story of Paul's adventures which we still have in our Bibles today.

### The friends go to Greece

One night, soon after he had met Luke, Paul had a dream. He saw a man from a place called Macedonia in Greece who begged him to go there to tell the Macedonians the good news of Jesus. Paul knew at once that this was what God wanted him to do. He and his friends got ready to leave immediately.

They sailed to Greece and made their way to a town called Philippi where they stayed for a few days. On the Sabbath they found a group of Jewish women praying by the river because there was no other meeting-place. Paul and Silas joined them and lost no time in telling them about Jesus.

One of the women, whose name was Lydia, believed and she was baptised. Lydia made her living selling the beautiful purple cloth which only the very rich people wore. She invited Paul and his friends to stay in her house while they were in Philippi.

### Paul and Silas in prison

Trouble was in store for Paul and Silas. A poor slave girl started to follow them around. She could tell people's fortunes, and her masters earned a lot of money from people who wanted to know what their futures would be. Whenever the girl saw Paul and Silas she would call, 'Here are two servants of the most high God!'

Paul was upset by this. He knew that the girl's powers came from an evil spirit and not from God. At last he could bear it no longer. Through the power of Jesus he freed her from the evil spirit and at once her magic powers left her.

The girl's masters were furious. They wouldn't be able to earn any more money. They grabbed hold of Paul and Silas and dragged them off to the city authorities. The two friends were beaten and then chained up in prison. But they knew God was with them still and they spent the night singing hymns of praise to him.

### The jailer

Suddenly, at about midnight, a violent earthquake shook the prison. Doors swung open and the chains fell off the prisoners. The jailer rushed in to find out what was happening. He was sure everyone had escaped and he drew his sword to kill himself, for he knew he would be blamed for losing the prisoners.

Paul saw what he was doing and shouted, 'Stop! Don't kill yourself! We're all here!'

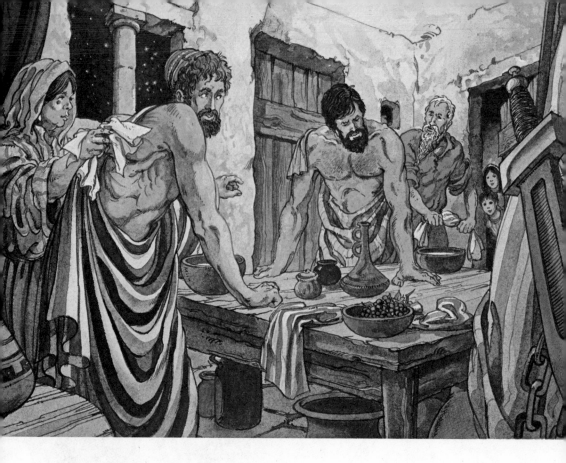

Amazed, the jailer dropped his sword and called for lights. He rushed into the cell and knelt trembling before Paul and Silas.

'What must I do now?' he asked.

They answered simply, 'Believe in Jesus and you and your family will be saved by God.'

At once the jailer took Paul and Silas to his home. He washed their wounds and they baptised him and all his family.

In the morning the authorities sent their men to the house to tell the jailer to let Paul and Silas go. To the jailer's surprise Paul was angry.

'I am a Roman citizen,' he said, 'and that means that I have special rights. A Roman citizen can't be arrested and punished without a trial, but you have beaten me and imprisoned me for no reason. Now you want me to go away and forget it. I won't go until you apologise!'

The authorities were frightened when they heard that Paul was a Roman citizen, and they apologised to him and asked him to leave the city. So, after saying goodbye to Lydia and the other new Christians, Paul and his friends travelled on to another big town called Thessalonica, seventy miles away.

## Trouble in Thessalonica

They spent three weeks there, and a number of people believed their message, including some Greeks who worshipped God in the Jewish way. Some of the leading women of the town were among them, but the synagogue leaders found it hard to believe in Jesus. They were so worried and upset by this new teaching that they stirred up a whole mob against Paul and his friends.

'We must hide!' exclaimed Paul, seeing the crowd come storming along the street looking for them. Paul, Silas, Luke and Timothy slipped quietly away. The crowd hammered on every door yelling for them to come out. The only person they could find was a man called Jason, who had had Paul staying in his house.

At once they dragged him off to the rulers of the town.

'This man's an enemy of the Roman Emperor!' they shouted. 'He follows another king called Jesus!'

The rulers were furious. Jason had no chance to explain. He had to pay a large fine before they would let him go. As soon as he was free he went to find Paul and his friends and helped them to escape from the town.

## Paul in Athens

Paul, Silas, Luke and Timothy made their way quickly to another city, Berea. The people there were friendly and listened eagerly to their teaching about Jesus. But danger still followed Paul. His enemies came after him and tried to turn the people of Berea against him. His friends said, 'You must try to get away, Paul. We'll stay and help the new Christians.'

'All right. I'll head towards the coast as though I'm going to find a ship, but really I'll go to Athens,' Paul decided.

'It's such a famous city you must speak for Jesus there,' the others agreed. 'We'll come and join you as soon as we can.'

So Paul went to Athens. While he waited for Silas and Timothy to join him there, he spent his time looking round the city. When he noticed the hundreds of statues of different gods and goddesses which the people worshipped, Paul wanted to tell them about the true God.

The Athenians enjoyed discussing ideas of all kinds, so they were interested to hear Paul. They asked him to come and talk to their city council. Paul went gladly. He told them about Jesus who had come to die so that their wrong-doings could be forgiven. He told them how God had raised Jesus from the dead. Some people believed Paul, but many of them laughed at him. They thought he was talking nonsense.

'Who is this idiot?' they asked.

Paul didn't mind. He knew that following Jesus was more important than being thought clever.

### Priscilla and Aquila

Paul soon moved on to the busy port of Corinth, just north of Athens. Here he made friends with a Jew called Aquila and his wife Priscilla. Aquila was a tent maker, and as Paul had learned the same trade when he was a boy, he stayed with them and helped them with their work. Together they sat and stitched the heavy tents.

By now Silas, Timothy and Luke had rejoined Paul. They went all over Corinth, teaching the people about Jesus. They stayed there for a year and a half, talking to anyone who would listen and helping the new believers to follow Jesus in a city where most people worshipped other gods.

As usual the Jewish leaders tried to stop Paul. They went to the

Roman governor of Corinth to complain about him. This time though, the governor was on Paul's side.

'If Paul had committed a crime I would have done something about it,' he said, 'but this is something you must settle yourselves!'

So Paul was able to go on speaking freely about Jesus.

'It's been very good here,' he said one day. 'But I must get back to Jerusalem.'

'We'll come with you as far as Ephesus,' said Priscilla and Aquila. 'That's going to be our new home.'

So the friends set sail and travelled together as far as Ephesus. Paul didn't stay long there. He wanted to get back to Jerusalem as quickly as he could. He did visit one synagogue, though, and preach about Jesus there. Many of the people who heard him begged him to stay and tell them more, and Paul promised to come back.

His ship took him as far as the

large port of Caesarea close to Joppa, and from there he travelled by land to Jerusalem where the leaders of the Christians lived. He had plenty of exciting news to tell them!

Then he went home to Antioch and spent some time with his friends there.

## Paul's third journey

Before long, however, he decided it was time to be travelling again. He set out to visit the new churches in the towns where he had first taught about Jesus. The Christians there were overjoyed to see him. They welcomed him warmly, and he encouraged them to be brave followers of Jesus.

At last he made his way to Ephesus as he had promised. Ephesus was a large town with a splendid temple to the goddess Diana which people came from many miles away to see. Some of the people who lived there had already become Christians, but most of them worshipped the Roman gods, and many practised

magic. They had heavy books of spells and little scrolls with charms written on them, which they used to carry with them to bring them luck.

When Paul arrived he began to teach the people about Jesus. He also healed many sick people in the name of Jesus and drove away evil spirits. Soon the people realised that Jesus was more powerful than any magic.

Some of the Christians who had practised magic realised that what they had been doing was wrong. They decided to have nothing more to do with it. Solemnly they brought their books and scrolls to the market place and made a huge bonfire. Thousands of valuable books were burnt up. News of this soon spread, and more people came to believe in Jesus because of it.

### Riot in Ephesus

There were many silversmiths in Ephesus who earned money by making models of the goddess Diana and her temple. After Paul had been there three years, they grew worried.

'If things go on like this,' they grumbled, 'there'll be nobody praying to Diana any more. They'll all be following Jesus and we'll be out of a job!'

When the townspeople heard

this they were furious and they began to shout, 'Long live Diana! Long live Diana!'

They found two of Paul's friends and dragged them off to the theatre where the public meetings were held. For two hours the people chanted and shouted. Nobody could calm them down. Paul wanted to go to try, but his friends wouldn't let him. It was too dangerous. At last the town clerk managed to make himself heard.

'We all know that our goddess Diana is great and powerful. Nobody disputes that. But you have brought these men here although they have done nothing criminal. If you have any complaints, make them in the law courts. Don't get Ephesus a bad name by causing a riot!'

The crowd listened to the town clerk and went home without making any more trouble. But Paul knew it was no longer safe for him to stay there.

He left Ephesus and travelled on to visit more of the churches he had helped to start on his first journeys. Then, after several months, Paul decided to go back to Jerusalem.

## Eutychus

On the way he and his friends stopped at the port of Troas. They stayed with the Christians who lived there, and on their last evening they all met together to worship God. The meeting was held in a room at the top of a tall building and it was crowded.

People sat close together on the floor or perched on the window sills. Smoky oil lamps hung from the ceiling and the air was stuffy and warm. Paul began to talk — he had so much to say before he left! One of the boys, called Eutychus, who was sitting on the window sill, began to doze. His head slipped back, and, before anyone could help him, he slid backwards through the window and crashed to the ground.

His friends rushed downstairs, but he was dead.

'Don't worry!' Paul put his arms round Eutychus as he spoke. 'Look! He's alive!'

Sure enough, Eutychus opened his eyes and then got to his feet. Overjoyed, his friends helped him upstairs again, and there they stayed until morning, praising God and listening to Paul's message.

### Paul says goodbye to the Ephesians

The journey back to Jerusalem took Paul near Ephesus again, but he did not want to lose time by stopping there. Instead he sent a message to the leaders of the church asking them to meet him at the port where the boat was docked. When they arrived he spoke solemnly to them.

'I don't know what will happen to me in Jerusalem. God has warned me to expect trouble and imprisonment wherever I go, but

that doesn't worry me! All I want is to finish the work God has given me to do: telling everyone I can, the good news about Jesus. So please pray for me; and keep on following Jesus yourselves.'

Then Paul and the leaders knelt

and prayed together. Sadly they said goodbye. They knew they would never see Paul again.

### Agabus' message

The ship carried Paul and his friends on across the sea. Once again they called at the port of Caesarea. This time they stayed with Philip who had baptised the Queen of Ethiopia's treasurer. He had four daughters who were all followers of Jesus.

While they were staying with Philip a man called Agabus arrived. God's Holy Spirit told him that Paul's life was in danger. Agabus tried to warn him. He took Paul's long belt and tied his own hands and feet with it.

'The Jews in Jerusalem will tie up the owner of this belt like this and then they'll hand him over to the Romans!' he said.

At once everyone begged Paul not to go to Jerusalem. Some people even had tears in their eyes as they pleaded with him to stay. But Paul said, 'You mustn't cry like that. You're breaking my heart. Don't you see that I'm ready to die for my Lord Jesus?'

They tried even harder to persuade him to change his mind, but he refused to listen. At last they gave up.

'We must leave it all to the Lord,' they said. 'He is in control; and we must do what he wants because that is best.'

# PAUL THE PRISONER

### Paul in danger

At last Paul reached Jerusalem. The Christians there welcomed him warmly, but they were worried for they knew Paul had many enemies there. And it was not long before his enemies attacked him.

Some of them spotted Paul in the streets with a friend from Ephesus. When they next saw Paul he was in the temple where only Jewish men were allowed to be. At once they decided that he had brought his Ephesian friend with him.

'Kill him!' they yelled. 'He's defying our sacred laws by

bringing foreigners into our most holy place!'

## Paul is arrested

At once a crowd gathered and dragged Paul out of the temple. They hit and kicked him, shouting angrily as they did so. Then someone told the commander of the Roman soldiers in Jerusalem that there was a riot. Quickly he took some men and marched to the temple. He stopped the crowd beating Paul and had him arrested. The soldiers had to hoist him up on their shoulders and carry him away to keep the crowd from tearing him apart. Paul tried to explain to the crowd about Jesus, but they wouldn't listen.

The Roman commander could not understand what Paul had done to enrage the crowd. He ordered his men to beat Paul until he told them. So the soldiers stripped Paul and tied him to a post. Then Paul calmly told them that he was a Roman citizen. They were breaking the law even by tying him up without giving him a fair trial first! Anxiously the commander questioned Paul. 'I had to buy my citizenship. It cost me a lot of money!' he said.

'I was born a Roman citizen!' Paul replied quietly.

Frightened, the commander had Paul's chains taken off him.

### Paul before the council

The commander still wasn't sure what Paul had done to make the Jews angry, so the next day he took Paul before the Jewish council.

Paul faced them calmly and began to explain what he had been doing.

At once the high priest ordered someone to hit him across the mouth.

Paul was angry. It was against the law to hit a prisoner.

'You hypocrite!' he shouted. 'You say that I've broken God's law but here you are doing the same yourselves!'

'Don't you know that you're talking to the high priest?' said the people standing near him.

Paul apologised. He knew that the law said that nobody should say bad things about the high priest.

'Brothers,' he called out, 'I've done nothing wrong. I'm on trial here simply because I believe that God will raise the dead to life!'

Now some of the council believed this, too, but others didn't. Both sides began to argue about what Paul had said. They grew so angry that the Roman

commander was frightened that they would tear Paul to pieces between them, and he ordered his soldiers to drag Paul to safety.

That night Paul saw Jesus standing beside his bed.

'Don't be afraid, Paul!' said Jesus. 'You have spoken bravely about me here in Jerusalem, and you must do the same in Rome, too!'

Paul's greatest wish had always been to speak for Jesus in Rome, the great city where the Emperor ruled. Now, perhaps through this trouble, his wish would be fulfilled. In spite of everything he felt happy.

### The plot

'Paul thinks he's safe now he's with the Romans, but we'll get him yet,' muttered his enemies. They vowed not to eat or drink until they had killed him.

'We'll ask the chief priests to

send Paul to them for further questioning, and we'll kill him on the way there,' they plotted.

They didn't see the little boy who crouched in the shadows and heard every word. He was Paul's nephew! Quietly he slipped away to the fort to warn his uncle.

At once Paul called an officer who took the boy to the commander.

The commander led the boy to a quiet corner.

'What do you have to tell me, son?' he asked.

When he heard the boy's story he sent him home, telling him not to breathe a word to anyone. Then he ordered two hundred foot soldiers, seventy horsemen and two hundred spearmen to get ready to take Paul out of Jerusalem as soon as it got dark.

'Take him down to Caesarea and let Governor Felix deal with the case!'

The commander wrote a letter to Felix about Paul: 'The Jews were about to kill this man, but I found out that he was a Roman citizen, so I stepped in to save his life. He seems to have broken some Jewish

law. I can't find him guilty of any crime against Rome. The Jews are still plotting against him, so I am sending him to you.'

It wasn't quite the truth, but it would never do for Governor Felix to find out that he had put a Roman citizen in chains and nearly had him beaten!

Paul left Jerusalem safely, surrounded by armed men. He knew God was looking after him.

### Paul goes before Felix

Five days later the high priest and other Jewish leaders hurried to Caesarea to tell Felix their side of the story.

'We want your excellency to know that the prisoner Paul is a most dangerous man. He has travelled all over the Empire starting riots among the Jews,' they said. 'He came to Jerusalem, but we arrested him in the temple when he was about to stir up more trouble there.'

'I went to the temple to pray, not to start trouble!' replied Paul. 'I worship God, just as these men do, but I follow Jesus, too. I am on trial here because I tell everyone that God raised Jesus from the dead.'

Felix decided to take an easy way out. 'I'll hear Paul's case later!' he said.

He hoped, too, that if he left Paul in prison for long enough Paul would give him some money in order to be set free. So Felix never gave Paul another trial. He kept him closely guarded, but allowed his friends to visit him.

### The new governor

At last, after two whole years, a new governor took over from Felix. The new governor, whose name was Festus, wanted to please the Jews, so he asked Paul to go to Jerusalem for another trial. Paul knew he would be killed if he set foot in the city.

'I am a Roman citizen,' Paul pleaded. 'I've done nothing wrong. There's no truth in any of the charges the Jewish leaders have brought against me. I want the Roman Emperor to try me. I appeal to have my case transferred to Rome!'

This was one of Paul's rights as a citizen, and Festus had to agree.

While arrangements were being made for Paul's journey, the king and queen of Judea arrived to welcome the new governor. Festus told them about Paul, and the king, Agrippa, asked to see him. The whole court gathered to hear his story. Eagerly, Paul told them all he had done to tell people everywhere about Jesus. 'Jesus is the special king God promised to us. He had to be punished and die, but God raised him from death,' he explained, but Festus interrupted: 'You're mad, Paul!' he cried, but King Agrippa wasn't so sure.

He talked to Paul a little longer, then he turned to Festus.

'If Paul hadn't appealed to Caesar you could have set him free,' he said. 'He has done nothing wrong.'

362

### Paul sets sail

It was late summer when Paul set sail for Rome, guarded by an officer called Julius. Two of Paul's friends, Luke and Aristarchus, travelled with him.

Julius could see that Paul was a good man, different from the

beginning to blow when they set out again. Once they reached Crete, Paul advised the ship's captain not to sail any further until winter was over.

However, both Julius and the captain were anxious to get to

dangerous criminals he often had to guard. He treated Paul well, and when the ship called at a port called Sidon, where Paul had friends, he allowed him to go to visit them. They were glad to see Paul, and gave him all sorts of useful things for the long voyage to Italy.

The autumn winds were

Rome, and they decided to press on with the journey.

Hardly had they left harbour when a furious storm blew up. The ship was thrown in all directions. Desperately the crew threw the cargo overboard to make the boat lighter, but still they could not get her under control. For two weeks they were driven by the storm.

Only Paul had any hope that they would be kept safe.

'God told me in a dream that we shall all reach Rome,' he said. 'I must stand my trial before Caesar. The ship will be lost, but God will protect us all.'

On the fourteenth night the sailors guessed that they were close to land. Frightened in case the ship drifted on to rocks, they dropped anchor and waited for dawn. Paul urged them to rest and eat. When they saw how calm he was, they were encouraged and had some food.

The first glimmer of dawn showed them a stretch of unknown coastline. Carefully the sailors tried to guide the boat towards the shore.

They didn't see the sandbank that blocked their way until the ship struck it! The boat was held fast while the pounding waves battered the stern.

The soldiers wanted to kill Paul and some other prisoners on board to stop them escaping in the confusion, but Julius stopped them. He ordered those who could swim to jump overboard and make for the shore. The rest were to use the broken planks from the ship as floats.

So it was that, as Paul had promised, everyone arrived safely on dry land.

### Paul and the snake

Once ashore they discovered that they were on the island of Malta. The weather was cold and it started to rain. The kindly islanders lit a huge bonfire for them, and Paul got busy gathering sticks. He was about to throw a bundle of wood on to the fire when a snake, brought out by the heat, coiled itself around his hand.

The islanders watched, horrified. 'This man is obviously a murderer! He's managed to escape the shipwreck, but he's doomed to die for his crimes,' they said.

But Paul shook the snake off and it fell into the fire. The islanders waited for him to swell up or drop dead, poisoned; when he didn't, they were very impressed. 'He must be a god,' they decided.

### The governor's father

It so happened that the island's chief official, a man called Publius, lived near the beach

where Paul and the others landed. Publius welcomed them warmly and invited them to stay with him, even though his father lay at home unwell.

'God rescued us, I'm sure he will cure your father!' Paul said.

He laid his hands on the old man and prayed. Publius' father recovered at once. The news spread all over Malta and many sick people came to Paul to be cured.

More impressed than ever, the grateful islanders brought Paul presents. When he set sail again, three months later, they loaded the ship with all sorts of useful things to replace what had been lost in the storm.

Paul and his friends reached Italy without any more adventures. They landed in a busy port and began the long journey to Rome by road. The news of their arrival reached the Christians in Rome, and they hurried out of the city to meet them. Paul was delighted at the welcome they gave him, and thanked God for bringing him to them safely.

Paul was still a prisoner. He was allowed to live in a rented house, but he had a soldier with him all the time to guard him. He could not leave the house, but many people came to visit him. He wrote letters to his friends in the many places he had visited, helping them with their problems, and encouraging them to follow the way of Jesus wherever they were.

## PAUL'S LETTERS

### *Onesimus*

'Master! Your runaway slave, Onesimus, has come back!' a breathless messenger rushed up to Paul's friend, Philemon. 'He's come all the way from Rome with a letter from Paul!'

'And what does he expect to get from me?' shouted Philemon angrily. 'A runaway slave deserves to be put to death. Bring him here at once!'

Onesimus came in, holding out a letter from Paul. Philemon broke the seal and unrolled the scroll. Suddenly he remembered the words of Jesus: 'Forgive those who wrong you...' Philemon was a follower of Jesus and many Christians who lived nearby came to worship God in his beautiful home. His anger began to cool.

'Brother Philemon,' wrote Paul. 'I thank God for you every time I pray.' Philemon softened. He read on.

'Onesimus has become a Christian too. He is like a son to me now. He has been a great help to me in prison. I should like to keep him here to help me, but he belongs to you. If he has stolen anything I will pay it back. You see, he is much more than a slave to you now. He is a Christian brother. Please welcome him back, just as if he were me. I am sure you will do what I ask; in fact I know you will do even more.'

Philemon thought of Paul chained up in prison. He reread the letter thoughtfully. Finally he turned to Onesimus waiting quietly beside him. 'Welcome home!' he said, and held out his arms.

## Parents and children

'Children,' Paul wrote in one of his letters, 'obey your parents. It's the right thing to do. It is one of the commandments God gave long ago and it has a promise to go with it. "If you obey your parents all will go well with you."

'Parents,' he continued, 'don't

nag at your children or keep threatening them. You will only make them resentful and angry. Instead, bring them up lovingly with positive suggestions. Correct them when it's necessary. Above all, teach them about Jesus.'

### The great race

Paul watched from his window. In the street, a crowd cheered a young athlete who had just won a race. On his head was his prize — a crown of green leaves. Paul thought about the races he had watched when he was free. He remembered how eagerly the athletes tried to win crowns, training for months beforehand, thinking about nothing but the games.

Smiling to himself, Paul went back to the letter he was writing.

'Following Jesus is like running a race in the arena,' he wrote. 'I don't want to be disqualified or left behind. I press on, running hard to win the prize which God will give me. His prize doesn't wither and fade like a crown of leaves. It lasts for ever. His prize is being with Jesus and sharing in his glory. You must run this race, too. Get into training now, and run well to win the prize.'

## A letter to Timothy

Paul had been in prison a long time. Some of his friends deserted him. Some left him to work in other cities. Only Luke stayed with him. Paul longed to see his old friends. He wrote to his young helper, Timothy, who was working in Ephesus.

'Do your best to come to see me, and get Mark to come with you, too, because I know he will help me. Call in at Troas for the cloak I left there: it gets cold here in Rome in the winter! And bring my books and papers so that I can keep on working in prison. My life is nearly over. I have run the race, and I am waiting for my prize.'

When the letter arrived, Timothy read it quickly, glad to be of use to the old man he loved. As soon as he could, he collected his belongings and set off to find Mark, so that they could make the long journey to Rome together.

# THE WORK GOES ON

### The Christians in Rome

The soldier who guarded Paul sat in a corner of the busy lamplit room. As usual, all kinds of people crowded in to worship Jesus. Jews and Romans, Greeks and Asians, men, women, children and slaves all mixed freely together. The soldier had never seen anything like it before. He listened while they sang. 'Jesus died a cruel death on the cross,' they began softly. Their voices grew louder: 'But God raised him high. The whole world will bow before him because Jesus is the Lord who brings glory to God the Father.'

Their song echoed into the corners of the shadowy room, loud and triumphant.

'They must be able to hear it all over Rome,' thought the soldier. 'Soon everyone will know about this Jesus.'

He was right. Before long crowds would hear men, women and children singing praises to Jesus as they were led out to die for him, only thirty years after he himself had died and risen again. Paul himself would be among those who died, but the lessons he had taught about Jesus were to spread through the whole world.

# JOHN'S VISION

## John sees Jesus

Many Christians besides Paul were punished for being followers of Jesus. John, the fisherman who had been Jesus' friend when he was alive on Earth, was arrested by the Romans and sent away to live on the small island of Patmos. John was old now, and although the island looked lovely when the sun shone and ripened the grapes on the steep green hillsides, it was hard to live there alone. He could not see his friends or meet with other Christians to worship Jesus with them.

In spite of his troubles John still loved and worshipped the Lord Jesus. One day, when he was praying, God spoke to John. He heard a voice ring out behind him like a trumpet.

John turned round and saw Jesus standing close by, surrounded by seven golden candlesticks. His face shone like the sun, and his whole body blazed with light. In his right hand he held seven stars. John fell down at his feet.

'Don't be afraid,' Jesus said. 'I am the One who was there in the beginning and I shall still be there at the end of time. I was dead but now I am alive for ever.'

His voice flooded the quiet island like the roar of a foaming waterfall. 'These seven stars and the seven candlesticks stand for the churches in seven places. I have a message for each church. Write down everything you hear and see.'

So John wrote it all down.

## Letters to the churches

First John wrote messages to the seven churches, just as Jesus gave him the words.

'I know you haven't given up your faith,' he wrote to the first church, 'even though you have been badly treated. But some of you don't love me as much as you used to, and you've started to do wrong. Stop doing wrong and listen to my Holy Spirit. There is a beautiful tree in God's garden and I give its fruit to the people who win a victory for me.'

Jesus spoke to the other churches in the same way, warning them to be obedient and faithful so that they could share in his victory and joy.

He spoke sternly to the seventh church: 'You think you are strong and powerful and rich, but really you are weak and poor because you don't rely on me. Turn back to me. I shall give you everything you need. Look, I'm just outside your door. Can't you hear me knocking? Open the door and let me in, and we shall sit and enjoy a meal together.'

### God as King

After this, God showed John what heaven is like. A door stood wide open and John saw a royal throne. Someone sat there, someone whose face shone as though it were made of precious jewels. A rainbow curved round the throne, the person on the throne was so glorious and powerful that all John could see was dazzling flashes of lightning. He heard an endless rumble of thunder. He looked down and saw seven fiery torches flaming around the throne, reflected in a million darting gold pieces by what seemed to be a sea of purest glass stretching out in front of the throne.

Magnificent beings bowed before the throne where God sat. They sang all day and all night, never stopping, 'Holy, holy, holy is the Lord God, the only ruler of the world from before its beginning to beyond its end.'

Twenty four leaders took off their golden crowns and tossed them down in front of God, as a sign that he was their king. The singing went on and on, an endless 'thank you' to God. As John listened, he knew that no matter how hard the Roman Emperor or other rulers tried to hurt Christians, God really was in control and he always would be.

John wrote down everything that he heard and saw. He knew that the churches that were being attacked for worshipping Jesus would be made brave when they read how powerful and wonderful God is.

### The new Jerusalem

Finally, God showed John a new heaven and a new Earth.

He heard God's voice saying, 'Look, I am making everything new!' and he saw a beautiful bride on her way to her wedding. 'All the old sad things have vanished,' said the voice. 'God will wipe away your tears and dry your eyes. There is no death now, no sadness or crying or hurt.'

'Come, John,' said the angel. 'I will show you the bride whom Jesus loves.'

The angel took John to the top of a mountain and he saw a city just like Jerusalem, all lit up and shining. filled with God's glory. There was no temple there because God himself was in the middle of the city and Jesus was with him, brighter than the golden streets.

'I am the bright morning star,' said Jesus. 'I am coming soon.'

There was no night-time at all in the city, and its gates stayed wide open.

'Come,' said the bride, whose wedding party is for everyone.

'Come,' repeated the Holy Spirit, who helped John to see heaven.

'Come,' wrote John. 'Everyone come. Are you thirsty? Jesus is like a drink of cold water. Come, then, because all this is true, and Jesus says he is coming soon.

'Come soon, come very soon, Lord Jesus!' John finished his book.